JOHN WEBSTER

JOHN WEBSTER
A Critical Study

by

CLIFFORD LEECH

Senior Lecturer in English in the
University of Durham

BIP   BCL 88

HASKELL HOUSE PUBLISHERS Ltd.
Publishers of Scarce Scholarly Books
NEW YORK. N. Y. 10012
1970

First Published 1951

HASKELL HOUSE PUBLISHERS Ltd.
Publishers of Scarce Scholarly Books
280 LAFAYETTE STREET
NEW YORK. N. Y. 10012

Library of Congress Catalog Card Number: 78-143481

Standard Book Number 8383-0690-X

Printed in the United States of America

CONTENTS

*

Introduction: Life and Work

Chapter I

Chapter II

Chapter III

Introduction

LIFE AND WORK

1. Life

WE know almost nothing of John Webster's life beyond what his writings tell us. Mr. F. L. Lucas has devoted eight pages in his standard edition of Webster[1] to bringing together the few contemporary references to the playwright and the various conjectural identifications with recorded John Websters that have from time to time been made. It is fairly certain that he was born not earlier than 1570 and not much later than 1580; he may be the Johannes Webster, son and heir of Johannes Webster of London, who was admitted to the Middle Temple on 1 August 1598; he tells us in the preface to his *Monuments of Honour* that he was born free of the Merchant Taylors Company; he was probably dead by 7 November 1634, the licensing date of Heywood's *Hierarchy of the Blessed Angels*, which refers to him in the past tense.[2] Charles Gildon, in his *Lives and Characters of the English Dramatic Poets*, published in 1698, adds that he became parish clerk of St. Andrew's, Holborn, but this unsupported statement may be regarded with some suspicion. In

[1] *The Complete Works of John Webster*, edited by F. L. Lucas, 1927, i. 49–56. My debt to this edition will be increasingly apparent in the following pages, where references will be simply to "Lucas".

[2] Professor C. J. Sisson (*Lost Plays of Shakespeare's Age*, 1936, p. 102) does not agree that Heywood's use of the past tense implies Webster's death: he suggests that the poet is the John Webster who was buried at St. James's, Clerkenwell, on 3 March 1638.

JOHN WEBSTER

1654 T. Hall attacked John Webster, vicar of Mitton (1610–82), as *"the Quondam Player"*, and this has been taken as evidence that the poet was at one time an actor; but much weight cannot be given to a description which was based on a mistaken identity and was made twenty years after the poet's death.

Yet it is certain that Webster stood high in esteem among his contemporaries. We have record of his collaboration, at one time or another, with Munday, Middleton, Drayton, Dekker, Heywood, Ford and Rowley, and it appears likely that he joined with Massinger in *The Fair Maid of the Inn*. Heywood's *Hierarchy of the Blessed Angels*, listing some of the leading poets of the time, links Webster with Fletcher and describes them as "of that learned packe None of the mean'st". *The Duchess of Malfi* was printed in 1623 with commendatory verses from Middleton, Rowley and Ford, and Ford's claim for his fellow-worker is high:

> *Crowne Him a Poet, whom nor Rome, nor Greece,*
> *Transcend in all theirs, for a Master-peece.*

Webster himself wrote commendatory verses for publications by Munday, Heywood, S. Harrison and Henry Cockeram, addressing Munday as "my kinde friend" and Heywood as "beloved friend". We have an attack on him from Henry Fitzjeffrey of Lincoln's Inn, in *Certain Elegies done by Sundry Excellent Wits* (1617), in which his slowness at composition and his surlily critical temper are glanced at: a diverting picture is drawn of Webster in the throes of writing:

> *See how he drawes his mouth awry of late,*
> *How he scrubs: wrings his wrists: scratches his Pate.*

The other side of the picture is given by S. Sheppard in his epigram "*On Mr.* Websters *most excellent Tragedy, called the White Devill*", published in 1651 in *Epigrams theological, philosophical, and romantic.* This begins with a bold assertion:

> *Wee will no more admire* Euripides,
> *Nor praise the Tragick streines of* Sophocles,
> *For why? thou in this Tragedie hast fram'd*
> *All reall worth, that can in them be nam'd:*

and proceeds to commend Webster's grace in writing and his vividness of portraiture. The terms used are sometimes odd: "How pretty are thy lines!" is not the praise that we should give, nor should we use the word "fluent" for Webster's prose. But the epigram is remarkable as the solitary tribute to *The White Devil* before the Restoration.

Of the plays associated with Webster's name, three were acted on the Restoration stage and the two major tragedies have a prolonged stage history of some interest. But it was not until the time of Lamb and Hazlitt that he was again recognised as among the leading writers of English drama. Leaving few traces of himself in sixteenth- and seventeenth-century records, he suffered critical neglect for nearly two centuries.[1] The first collected edition of his plays was Dyce's, published in 1830. During the last hundred years his reputation has slowly risen, until to-day he joins that small band of Elizabethan and Jacobean writers whose plays live yet on the stage.

---

[1] Lucas's thirteen-page bibliography in vol. i of his edition does not contain a single eighteenth-century entry under the heading of "criticism".

JOHN WEBSTER

2. Writings

The following is a list of Webster's writings, including those doubtfully ascribed to him:

(a) Dramatic Writings

(i) Plays wholly by Webster

The White Divel, or, The Tragedy of Paulo Giordano Ursini, Duke of Brachiano, With The Life and Death of Vittoria Corombona the famous Venetian Curtizan, published in 1612. The date of composition is uncertain, but is probably later than 2 February 1609, when Jonson's *Masque of Queens* was produced: there is a clear allusion to the masque in III. ii.[1] The well-known address to the reader prefixed to the published version tells us that the play was performed in winter and to an unappreciative audience. The company was the Queen's Men, the theatre the Red Bull. The play was reprinted in 1631, 1665 and 1672. The quarto of 1631 describes the play as "*divers times Acted, by the Queenes Maiesties servants, at the Phoenix, in Drury Lane*"; that of 1665 as "*Acted (formerly by Her Majesties Servants) at the Phoenix in Drury Lane; And At This Present (by His now Majesties) at the Theatre Royal*"; that of 1672 as "*acted at the Theatre Royal, By His Majesties Servants*".

The Tragedy of the Dvtchesse of Malfy, printed in 1623. The title-page claims to present "The perfect and exact Coppy, with diuerse *things Printed, that the length of the Play would* not beare in the Presentment". The play must have been performed before

[1] Lucas, i. 67.

4

16 December 1614, when William Ostler, the first Antonio, died. We are told by the title-page that the play was acted by the King's Men *"priuatly, at the Black-Friers; and publiquely at the Globe"*. It appears that the play was revived in 1617, as an alteration near the beginning of the text, introducing a topical allusion, was certainly made at that time.[1] The first quarto gives two actors' names for the parts of Ferdinand, the Cardinal and Antonio. The play was reprinted in 1640, *c.* 1664, 1678 and 1708. The title-page of 1640 describes it as *"approvedly well acted at the Black-Friers"*; that of *c.* 1664 as *"Acted by his late Majesties Servants at Black Fryers with great Applause, Thirty Years since. And now Acted by his Highnesse the Duke of York's Servants"*; that of 1678 as *"now Acteed [sic] At The Dukes Theater"*; that of 1708 as *"Now Acted at the Queen's Theatre in the Hay-Market, By Her Majesties Company of Comedians"*.

The Deuils Law-case. Or, When Women goe to Law, the Deuill is full of Businesse, published in 1623. The probable date of first performance is *c.* 1620.[2] The title-page of the quarto tells us it "was approouedly well Acted by her Maiesties Servants". The theatre was the Red Bull.[3]

(ii) *Plays partly by Webster*

Induction to The Malcontent, published in 1604. Three editions of Marston's play appeared in that year: the title-page of the third reads: "The Malcontent. Augmented by *Marston*. With the additions played by the Kings, Maiesties servants. Written by

---

[1] Cf. below, p. 73. [2] Cf. Lucas, ii. 213–16.
[3] George Fullmer Reynolds, *The Staging of Elizabethan Plays At the Red Bull Theatre 1605–1625*, 1940, p. 21.

Ihon Webster." The play was originally acted by the
Children of the Queen's Revels at Blackfriars, and
was taken over by the King's Men, for whom the
induction was written and certain additions made
"to entertaine a little more time, and to abridge the
not received custome of musicke in our Theater".
Apart from the induction, the additions seem to be
the work of Marston.[1] Both the play and the induction were probably written in 1604 or shortly before
that.

The Famous History of Sir Thomas Wyat, published
in 1607. The title-page attributes the play to Dekker
and Webster. Henslowe records payment to Chettle,
Dekker, Heywood, Smith and Webster for a play
called *Lady Jane* on 15 and 21 October 1602.[2] The
actors were the Queen's Men. There was a second
quarto in 1612.

West-ward Hoe, published in 1607. The title-page
attributes the play to Dekker and Webster. The
generally accepted date is 1604.[3] The actors were
the Children of Paul's.

North-ward Hoe, published in 1607. The title-
page attributes the play to Dekker and Webster.
The probable date is 1605.[4] The actors were the
Children of Paul's.

A Cure for a Cuckold, published in 1661. The title-
page assigns it to Webster and Rowley, and says "it
hath been several times Acted with great Applause".
Francis Kirkman, in "The Stationer, to the Judicious
Reader", observes:

---

[1] Cf. Lucas, iii. 296–8; Sir Edmund Chambers, *The Elizabethan Stage*, 1923, iii. 431–2.
[2] Lucas, iii. 239. Cf. below, p. 54.
[3] *The Elizabethan Stage*, iii. 295.   [4] *Ibid.*, iii. 295–6.

As for this *Play*, I need not speak any thing in its Commendation, the Authors names, *Webster* and *Rowley*, are (to knowing men) sufficient to declare its worth: several persons remember the Acting of it, and say that it then pleased generally well; and let me tell you, in my judgement it is an excellent old *Play*.

The date of first acting was probably *c.* 1625.[1]

Appius and Virginia, published in 1654. The title-page assigns it to Webster alone, but Rupert Brooke and others have argued that Heywood's share in it was considerable.[2] The play is in Beeston's list of Cockpit plays in 1639.[3] Various dates of first performance have been suggested, ranging from 1603–4 to 1626–34: Mr. Lucas's conjecture is 1625–7.[4] The play was reprinted in 1659 and 1679. The 1679 quarto describes it as "Acted at the Duke's Theatre under the name of The Roman Virgin or Unjust Judge".[5]

(iii) *Plays conjecturally by Webster*

The Weakest Goeth to the Wall, published in 1600. Edward Phillips in *Theatrum Poetarum* (1675) assigned it to Webster and Dekker, along with three other plays of known (and different) authorship. Langbaine in 1691 dismissed these ascriptions as "a great mistake".[6]

The Thracian Wonder, published in 1661 along with *A Cure for a Cuckold*. Kirkman ascribed both plays to Webster and Rowley. The probable date of

[1] Lucas, iii. 3–4. [2] *Ibid.*, iii. 134–45.
[3] *The Elizabethan Stage*, iii. 508.
[4] Lucas, iii. 121–30. Cf. below, p. 94. [5] Cf. below, p. 14.
[6] Lucas, iv. 245; *The Elizabethan Stage*, iv. 52.

composition is *c.* 1600, and no one now takes Kirkman's ascription seriously.[1]

Additions to The Spanish Tragedy, published in 1602. It was Lamb who first suggested Webster's authorship for these additions. As Mr. Lucas points out, it is difficult to imagine Webster writing as well as this at the same time as he was contributing to *Sir Thomas Wyatt.*[2]

The Revenger's Tragedy, published in 1607, and now generally regarded as Tourneur's.[3] Fleay put forward the theory of Webster's authorship.[4]

Any Thing for a Quiet Life, published in 1662. The title-page assigns it to Middleton. Webster's part-authorship was first suggested by H. D. Sykes in 1921, and has been accepted by Mr. Lucas, who dates the play *c.* 1621.[5]

The Faire Maide of the Inne, published in 1647 in the Beaumont and Fletcher Folio. It was licensed as Fletcher's on 22 January 1626, but opinion has differed widely concerning its authorship. Mr. Lucas accepts the view of H. D. Sykes that the writing was shared by Massinger and Webster, with some contribution from Ford.[6] The writing was probably done in 1625.[7] The play was reprinted in the second Beaumont and Fletcher Folio of 1679.

(iv) *Lost Plays*

Caesar's Fall. Henslowe gave five pounds on 22 May 1602 to Munday, Middleton, Drayton, Webster "& the Rest" as an advance payment for

[1] Lucas, iv. 246–7; *The Elizabethan Stage,* iv. 49.
[2] Lucas, iv. 248–9.
[3] Cf. *The Works of Cyril Tourneur,* edited by Allardyce Nicoll, N.D., pp. 18–20.   [4] *The Elizabethan Stage,* iv. 42.
[5] Lucas, iv. 66–8.   [6] *Ibid.,* iv. 148–52.   [7] *Ibid.,* iv. 147.

this play. It is doubtless to be identified with a play called "too shapes", for which Henslowe gave Dekker, Drayton, Middleton, Webster and Munday a final payment of three pounds on 29 May 1602.[1]

Christmas comes but once a Year. Henslowe gave three pounds on 2 November 1602 to Heywood and Webster as an advance payment for this play. Later he made further payments for it to Chettle and Dekker.[2]

The Guise. This play is mentioned, along with *The White Devil* and *The Duchess of Malfi*, as among "my other Workes" in Webster's dedication to *The Devil's Law Case*, published in 1623. As it is mentioned after the two major tragedies, we can fairly assume that it was written 1614–23.

The Late Murder in Whitechapel, or Keep the Widow Waking. This play, bringing together two contemporary crimes, a matricide and an enforced marriage of a rich widow, was acted at the Red Bull in 1624. The performance led to a Star Chamber suit in 1625 and 1626. The play is doubtless to be identified with "A New Tragedy, called, A Late Murther of the Sonn upon the Mother: Written by Forde, and Webster", which was licensed in September 1624. The Star Chamber proceedings reveal that Dekker and Rowley were also concerned in the writing, and perhaps took the major share.[3]

(b) Non-dramatic Writings

Commendatory verses prefixed to the Third Part of Munday's translation of *Palmerin of England*, published in 1602.

Ode prefixed to S. Harrison's *Arch's of Triumph*,

[1] *Ibid.*, i. 53.   [2] *Ibid.*, i. 54.
[3] C. J. Sisson, *Lost Plays of Shakespeare's Age*, pp. 80–124.

JOHN WEBSTER

Erected in honour of . . . James the First, published in 1604.

Commendatory verses prefixed to Heywood's *Apology for Actors*, published in 1612.

A Monvmental Colvmne, Erected to the liuing Memory of the euer-glorious Henry, late Prince of Wales, published in 1613, licensed on 25 December 1612.[1] It was also published in *Three Elegies on the most lamented Death of Prince Henrie* (1613).

New Characters (Drawne to the life) of seuerall persons, in seuerall qualities, published in 1615. This consists of a group of thirty-two "characters" added, with a separate title-page, to the sixth edition of the Overbury collection. The case for Webster's authorship, based on the existence of parallel passages in the "characters" and Webster's plays, and on stylistic similarities, is reasonably convincing.[2]

Monuments of Honour, the London Lord Mayor's Show of 1624, printed in that year.

Verses forming part of an engraving, "The Progenie of the most Renowned Prince Iames King of Great Britaine France and Ireland". There are seven stanzas of verses, each on one of the royal figures shown in the engraving. According to the British Museum *Catalogue of Engraved British Portraits*, this is the second state of a print originally engraved in James I's lifetime: an apparent reference to Charles I's betrothal to Henrietta Maria seems to date the original print not earlier than December 1624. Beneath the verses are the words "Hæc composuit Ioannes Webster".[3]

[1] Lucas, iii. 268. [2] Cf. Lucas, iv. 6–14. See also below, pp.106–9.
[3] Bernard M. Wagner, "New Verses by John Webster", *Modern Language Notes*, xlvi (June 1931), 403–5.

3. Stage History

We have seen that three plays by Webster—*The White Devil*, *The Duchess of Malfi* and *Appius and Virginia*—were reprinted in Restoration times. A fourth, *A Cure for a Cuckold*, was printed for the first time in 1661, but we have no evidence of Restoration performance and we need not take Kirkman's commendation [1] as necessarily indicating that the play was in the theatrical repertory before the Civil War. The other three, however, come quickly into notice after the Restoration, and it is likely that all three were commonly offered in the London playhouses between the dates of first performance and 1642. The wording of the 1631 title-page to *The White Devil* [2] is in itself an indication that the bad initial reception at the Red Bull did not discourage the actors from trying the play again. The several seventeenth-century printings of both *The White Devil* and *The Duchess of Malfi* suggest a fairly continuous hold on the stage till the end of the century.

When the theatres reopened in 1660, there were few new plays available and arrangements were made for the two companies to share the pre-war dramatic repertory. *The Duchess of Malfi* was among the plays allotted to Davenant,[3] and we know that Pepys saw it on 30 September 1662 ("well performed, but Betterton and Ianthe [4] to admiration") and again on 25 November 1668.[5] Downes tells us:

[1] Cf. above, p. 7.   [2] Cf. above, p. 4.

[3] Allardyce Nicoll, *A History of Restoration Drama 1660–1700*, 1928, p. 314.   [4] *i.e.* Mary Saunderson, later Mrs. Betterton.

[5] *The Diary of Samuel Pepys*, ed. Wheatley, 1903–4, ii. 348, viii. 165.

11   B

JOHN WEBSTER

This Play was so exceeding Excellently *Acted* in all Parts; chiefly, Duke *Ferdinand* and *Bosola*: It fill'd the House 8 Days Successively, it proving one of the Best of Stock Tragedies.[1]

We have record of a revival at Whitehall Palace on 13 January 1686.[2] The title was changed to *The Unfortunate Duchess of Malfy* for the edition of 1708, and the play had been given under that name at the Haymarket on 22 July 1707.[3] The stressing of the pathetic note in the title is significant: the play was a generation later to undergo its first metamorphosis [4] into a sentimental melodrama, and already in 1707 an attempt is made to suggest a similarity of style between Webster and Otway or Southerne. In the 1708 edition we have the following note after the list of dramatis personae:

Note, Those Lines which were omitted in the Acting, by reason of the length of the Play, are marked with (").

[1] John Downes, *Roscius Anglicanus*, ed. Summers, N.D., p. 25. This evidence of Restoration popularity would be confirmed by Montague Summers' observation that in Rawlins' *Tom Essence, or The Modish Wife* (1677) the scene of IV. ii is described as "Malfey's Chamber" (*The Restoration Theatre*, 1934, p. 217; *Roscius Anglicanus*, p. 185): I can, however, find no trace of this in the British Museum copy of the play.

[2] Allardyce Nicoll, *A History of Restoration Drama 1660–1700*, p. 312.

[3] Genest, *Some Account of the English Stage*, 1832, ii. 374.

[4] According to Samuel A. Tannenbaum, *John Webster (A Concise Bibliography)*, (*Elizabethan Bibliographies*, No. 19), New York, 1941, p. 2, *The Duchess of Malfi* was first adapted by R. Baron as *Gripus and Hegio; or, The Passionate Lovers* in 1647. But this pastoral playlet, which occurs in a courtly romance called Ἐροτοπαίγνιον *Or The Cyprian Academy*, is in no sense an adaptation of Webster: it has, however, a number of speeches taken almost verbatim from *The Duchess of Malfi*.

The passages so marked are fairly frequent, but we must remember that the original edition of 1623 also included "diuerse *things Printed, that the length of the Play would* not beare in the Presentment". The passages in quotation marks in 1708 thus merely bear witness to the continuing inability of the playhouse to cope with the length of Webster's play. It is perhaps more important to note that the 1708 edition could silently omit altogether a number of passages in the original text: III. iv (the scene at Loretto) is omitted entirely,[1] and there are things missing here and there throughout the play.[2]

The White Devil was revived soon after the Restoration by the King's Company under Killigrew. Pepys saw it on 2 October 1661, but "coming late, and sitting in an ill place, I never had so little pleasure in a play in my life".[3] Two days later he visited the theatre again, "and saw a bit of 'Victoria', which pleased me worse than it did the other day".[4] Downes includes the play in a list of "Old Plays . . . Acted but now and then; yet being well Perform'd, were very Satisfactory to the Town":[5] this list covers the years immediately following the opening of the Drury Lane theatre in 1663. The title-pages of the

---

[1] We must assume that this scene was given in Jacobean times, as we know that a song was provided by another hand than Webster's: the original text has a marginal note, "The Author disclaimes this Ditty to be his". The players would hardly have gone to the trouble of obtaining the song (which clearly Webster did not much admire) if they had no intention of playing the scene.

[2] *e.g.* in Antonio's speech on the French court at the beginning of I. i, and the reference to the "naked sword" in "the old tale" at the end of the scene.

[3] *The Diary of Samuel Pepys*, ii. 114.

[4] *Ibid.*, ii. 116. [5] *Roscius Anglicanus*, p. 9.

1665 and 1672 editions tell us that *The White Devil*
was being acted in these years. Langbaine in 1691
asserted that *The White Devil*, *The Duchess of Malfi*
and *Appius and Virginia* "have even in our Age gain'd
Applause".[1]

We know much less of the Restoration stage-
career of *Appius and Virginia*, but the dearth of in-
formation suggests that the play did not last long.
Apparently it was the first of Webster's plays to be
adapted to post-1660 taste, for the Bodleian copy of
the 1679 edition has this fly-leaf note by Malone:

Langbaine says he was told by Cartwright the comedian
that this play of Webster's was altered by Betterton on its
revival at the Duke's Theatre. This therefore is Betterton's
alteration. The original edition was printed in 1654. M.

In his *Account of the English Dramatic Poets* Langbaine gives the following note on the play:

4⁰. *Lond.* 1659. I suppose there may be an older Edition
than mine; but this is that which was acted at the Duke's
Theatre, and was alter'd (as I have heard by Mr. *Carth-
wright*) by Mr. *Betterton*.[2]

Mr. Lucas has pointed out that the 1659 and 1679
editions are merely re-issues of the original text,
though it may well be true that Betterton adapted the
play for the presentation referred to on the 1679
title-page.[3] In any event, we cannot know either the
nature or the extent of Betterton's alterations. The
adaptation had apparently been made as early as

[1] Gerard Langbaine, *An Account of the English Dramatic Poets*,
1691, p. 508.
[2] *Ibid.*, p. 509.　　　[3] Lucas, i. 10. Cf. above, p. 7.

12 May 1669, when Pepys saw *The Roman Virgin*, "an old play", at Lincoln's Inn Fields.[1]

In the early eighteenth century both *The White Devil* and *The Duchess of Malfi* fell into the adapter's hands. In 1707 there was published *Injur'd Love: or, The Cruel Husband. A Tragedy. Design'd to be Acted at the Theatre Royal. Written by Mr. N. Tate, Author of the Tragedy call'd King Lear*. In impertinence the play does not fall short of its title-page. It begins with an archly moralising prologue, which expresses the view that no Brachianos are now to be found, and proceeds to rebuke unfaithful husbands both in the city and among people of fashion: let them learn fidelity from "Virtuous Ladies", a "Pious Court" and "*our* Reforming Play". The epilogue takes up this strain, and urges that Brachiano's end should "*fright Ill-natur'd Husbands to their Wits*". Neither prologue nor epilogue mentions Webster's name, but the play is described in the epilogue as not "*a slight New-fashion'd PLAY*", but

> *a Vessel that would bear the shock*
> *Of Censure; Yes, old Built, but Heart of Oak.*

Tate was ready to assure the audience that he could give them thin modern stuff if he cared, and indeed this 1707 vintage makes *The White Devil* as thin a potation as could well be managed.

From the evidence of the title-page we can assume that the play was not acted,[2] and the printed text shows many signs of insufficient care in the adaptation. The list of dramatis personae confuses Julio and Lodovico, and omits various minor parts. Below

[1] *The Diary of Samuel Pepys*, viii. 322.
[2] Genest, x. 152, lists it among "Plays Printed, but not Acted".

15

we read: "SCENE, *ROME*", but Acts IV and V take place at Padua. At the end of II. i Francisco tells Brachiano "you may grace The Tryal with your Presence", but in II. ii—the arraignment of Vittoria —Tate preserves Monticelso's rebuke to Brachiano: "here is no Place assign'd you". In III. ii Antonio and Gasparo are given an entry when they are apparently already on the stage. Francisco is ignorant of Isabella's death in III. iii, yet Lodovico had knowledge of it in the previous scene. In IV. i Marcello is described first as older than Flamineo and then as younger. In V. ii Flamineo announces his intention of drawing the traverse to see Cornelia's lamentations over Marcello, but he is apparently interrupted by the appearance of Brachiano's ghost: after the ghost's departure, Flamineo refers to "the piteous sight of my dead Brother; and my Mother's Dotage".

Professor Hazelton Spencer has noted the workings of Restoration prudery in the adaptations of Shakespeare.[1] Tate, whose version of *King Lear* had appeared in 1681, was likely twenty years later to cultivate even more strenuously a modesty of utterance. So, in taking over Lodovico's cry in I. i:

> *Ile make Italian cut-works in their guts*
> *If ever I returne,*

he changes "guts" to "Skinns". In II. ii (the arraignment), the word "whore" is generally replaced by "harlot", and "bawd" by "minion". In V. i (corresponding to Webster's V. iii), the dream-narratives of Zanche and Francisco (Lodovico in Tate) are much expurgated. Anything, moreover, that could be taken as profanity is softened or excised: at Brachiano's

[1] *Shakespeare Improved*, 1927, pp. 150, 236, *et al.*

death the references to church matters are few, there are no Latin prayers, no holding of the crucifix before the dying man, and the compelling words of Webster:

Strangle him in private. What! will you call him againe
To live in treble torments? for charitie,
For Christian charitie, avoid the chamber,

are feebly reduced to "O for Charity, for Charity avoid the Chamber". It is significant in this connection that the English Ambassador's words in the trial scene, "Trew, but the Cardinals too bitter", are given by Tate to the Spanish Ambassador: Tate had no wish to enlist our sympathies against Monticelso, as Webster was impelled to despite a recognition of the prisoners' guilt.[1] Nor could Tate wish to throw doubts on the rightness of Francisco's revenge: he omits therefore Monticelso's attempt to dissuade Lodovico from the undertaking and Francisco's trick to convince Lodovico of Monticelso's hypocrisy. For Tate, as for other writers of "tragedy" in the Restoration and early eighteenth century, the issues of right and wrong were almost always to be presented as crystal clear.

Nevertheless, there is a good deal of confusion in the total effect made by this version. Tate made a half-hearted attempt to whitewash Vittoria herself. In the first encounter with Brachiano, in I. ii, she is given an aside:

Yes I will meet him, but for other Ends
Than their vile Purposes.

We are presumably meant to believe her innocent of adultery and murder, and the scene in which she so cleverly gets Brachiano to the point of marriage, in

[1] Cf. below, p. 38.

the house of convertites, disappears. Her final words
in the play—"O my greatest sinne lay in my blood.
Now my blood paies for't"—are omitted too. Yet her
innocence is not continuously obvious, and at times
Tate leaves in a passage, such as that where Vittoria
and Zanche tread on the apparently dead Flamineo,
which is hardly consonant with the picture of a
slandered virtue that he apparently intended. Professor Hazelton Spencer has linked Tate's version
with the "she tragedies" of John Banks,[1] but the
adapter, in straining after a merely pathetic effect,
has found his Jacobean material intractable. He has,
however, tried to heighten the virtue of other characters besides Vittoria: in his IV. i, corresponding
to Webster's V. i, it is only Marcello, and not Cornelia, who strikes Zanche; Isabella is made much
more pathetic in her scene with Brachiano, and even
the little Giovanni is brought in at this point to
sharpen the effect.

The alterations are not all in the directions of
sentiment and decorum. Tate does at times write in
the Restoration huffing mode: when Brachiano tells
Isabella "Our Sleeps are sever'd", we have stage
directions for "*A Noise under Ground*" and "*Light-
ning and Thunder*", and when Brachiano is poisoned
Antonio and Gasparo end IV. ii in this way before
they go to complete their task at his death-bed:

ANT. *We have struck mortally this royal Stag.*
GASP. *Let's follow to his Bay.*
ANT. *And see him worry'd by his own Quack Dogs.*
GASP. *And wash our Hands in's Gore.*
LUD. *O 'twill compleat the Sport.*   [*Exeunt.*

[1] "Tate and *The White Devil*", *ELH*, i (1934), 235–49.

With such passages we should associate those touches, more at home in Restoration comedy, which not infrequently find their way into the heroic drama and its succession: the plotting in Act IV in Brachiano's court at Padua goes on to the accompaniment of a masked ball, and we find Zanche, masked, testing Flamineo's constancy. So, too, the last scene of all opens, astonishingly, with a song: its text is not given, but one would be hard put to it to imagine any song that would not destroy the tension at this point, when Flamineo is coming to Vittoria and Zanche armed with the bogus instruments of death.

Lewis Theobald, the first adapter of *The Duchess of Malfi*, had the satisfaction of seeing his work actually on the stage. It was published in 1735 as *The Fatal Secret. A Tragedy. As it is Acted at the Theatre-Royal, In Covent-Garden. By Mr. Theobald.* Like Tate, Theobald apparently saw no reason to give Webster's name on his title-page, and indeed in a letter to Warburton of 18 December 1731 he sketches out the play and gives extracts, without a mention of Webster, even though he incorporates some of Webster's lines in the passages that he quotes.[1] However, the present tense used on the title-page disguises the fact that the adaptation met with the fate it deserved: in his preface, Theobald refers to the play having pleased its audience *"two Years ago in the Representation"*, but goes on to admit that it was *"prais'd and forsaken"* because, he tells us, the town was in a political ferment and consequently inattentive. Like Tate, Theobald aimed at producing

[1] B. L. Joseph, "Lewis Theobald and Webster", *Comparative Literature Studies*, xvii–xviii (1945), 29–31.

a pathetic drama which would especially please the
ladies of the audience:

If the Piece has any Praise, it is, in my Opinion, that it
had Power to draw Tears from fair Eyes. The Poet, who
writes for the Stage, should principally aim at pleasing his
female Judges: for the best Proof, whether he can draw a
Distress, is, how far their Nature and Virtues are touch'd
with his Portrait.

It was unfortunately true that *The Duchess of Malfi*
lent itself to this kind of perversion more readily
than *The White Devil*.

The list of dramatis personae prepares us for the
worst. Included is the "*Young Duke of* Malfy, *about*
12 *Years old*", played by "Miss Binckes". Among
the other changes, we note the absence of Julia, the
Cardinal's mistress, not to be easily assimilated to
the new mode.

To some extent Theobald's changes are in the
interest of "regularity". The scene is Malfi throughout, and the time of the action is shortened: the play
opens with Delio, not Antonio, arriving from France
and hearing from his friend that he has secretly
married the Duchess that morning. Moreover, Theobald administers strict poetic justice. Ferdinand and
the Cardinal die, but the Duchess and Antonio are
spared. Antonio is intended to be a more vigorous
figure than in Webster: in the scene in the Duchess's
bed-chamber corresponding to Webster's III. ii, he
interrupts Ferdinand's threats to the Duchess, and
Ferdinand says he would kill him at once had not
Antonio once saved his life in battle; and though
Antonio agrees to leave the Duchess and flee to
Ancona, he and Delio return disguised as pilgrims

almost at once. Theobald also prepares the way for
Ferdinand's madness by inserting in Act III a
statement that he had previously suffered from
lycanthropy.

But these structural changes are incidental. Theobald was concerned not merely to regularise Webster
but to transform the play into an acceptable vehicle
for pathos. The terror of it is exorcised. In Act IV
Ferdinand gives the Duchess Antonio's ring, not a
dead man's hand; he tells her Antonio is dead, with
no waxwork show to chill the blood; her strangling is
to be done off-stage, and her statue is placed in a
coffin to convince Ferdinand that the execution has
been done.[1] There are no children killed, and Miss
Binckes as the young Duke was able to bless a re-
united mother and stepfather, when Bosola produced
the Duchess and Antonio removed his disguise after
the deaths of Ferdinand and the Cardinal.

In Act II Bosola is made to echo *Macbeth*, beginning a soliloquy "I'm here in double trust", but generally Theobald is dependent on his own resources
in language or on such of Webster's words as he
cares to leave untouched. Wherever he alters, he
flattens. Bosola's perhaps too provocative image—

*We are meerely the Starres tennys-balls (strooke and banded
Which way please them)—*

is given by Theobald to Ferdinand, for Bosola is

[1] The contrivance of this "happy ending" was clearly suggested
by Ferdinand's reproach to Bosola in Webster's IV. ii:

*Why didst not thou pitty her? what an excellent
Honest man might'st thou have bin
If thou hadst borne her to some Sanctuary!*

repentant and must not be impious, and is turned into a lilting commonplace:

> *Man's but the Tennis-ball of Fate, and bandy'd*
> *Which way it pleases.*

The Duchess's last words—

> *Go tell my brothers, when I am laid out*
> *They then may feede in quiet—*

become:

> *When I am dead,*
> *My vengeful Brothers then may sleep in Quiet.*

For Theobald, "laid out" and "feede" were words insufficiently refined. And, at first sight most astonishingly, the most famous line in Webster becomes:

> *Cover her Face; my Eyes begin to dazzle.*

The alteration to this line gives us perhaps a clue to the whole problem. Not only Tate and Theobald laid hands on the Jacobeans: Dryden's stature is not to be questioned, yet he wrote *Troilus and Cressida; or, Truth Found Too Late*, turning Shakespeare's play into a romantic "tragedy" with Cressida ever faithful and Troilus dying a hero's death. The explanation is not simply one of insensitivity, or of the mechanical observance of rules or current fashion. The tragedy of the Jacobeans contemplated the darkness, the great cold which they felt to encompass man's everyday existence: their preoccupation with pain and mental anguish came from no mere desire to make the flesh creep, but rather from a sharp recognition of man's weakness and solitude. With that they had also a lively sense of wonder at the functioning of

man's body: copulation or excretion could be a jest,
but the comedy was cosmic. And above all, they
marvelled at human frenzies, at love and at ambition
and at the lust for blood. After the Civil War and the
Interregnum, these attitudes of mind were suppressed. The Jacobeans wrote without a full consideration of what their plays implied: the men of
the Restoration had learned to be analytic, to explore
their own purposes. Bawdry was well enough and
could be excused for its entertainment value, but a
too disturbing passion was to be reprobated, as in
Congreve's Lady Touchwood, or made into matter
for laughter, as in Wycherley's Pinchwife. Poetic
justice was necessary, for a hint that things might go
ultimately awry would disorder the whole framework
of belief. Almanzor, then, must win his Almahide,
and Tate's Lear and Cordelia be preserved for happi-
ness. Sometimes, of course, a play might end in
disaster. Otway's Monimia or Southerne's Isabella
drew tears in their last anguish. Dryden's Antony
and Addison's Cato marched to a climax of death.
But in these instances we find either an absence of
universal implication—so that Otway and Southerne
and Rowe seem concerned only with an individual's
distress—or an assurance that after all things are for
the best: the world is well lost for love, and the death
of Cato can arouse admiration without terror, can
provide an example of fortitude with no hint of
cosmic wrong.

Exceptionally, of course, men could turn aside
from the path of conformity, but their deviations
were not likely to find a welcome in the theatre.
Gulliver had been written before Theobald adapted
The Duchess of Malfi, but what the solitary reader

might exceptionally admire would hardly win tolera-
tion from a group-audience. The Restoration disliked
"an honest Satire against our crying Sin", as Dryden
described *Limberham* in explaining its failure on the
stage, and *The Double Dealer* was no favourite of the
town. Wycherley's Manly lashed the times, but his
rage dissolved into sentiment. The dramatists might
aspire to satire and strength, but the town kept them,
most often, to wit. The theatre was no place for the
more deeply disturbing kinds of drama. Old plays
might be put into becoming order, and *Lear* or
Timon made easily presentable. We have seen that
Webster's two major tragedies survived into the
Restoration period with little change, but their existence was a perpetual challenge which in time Tate
and Theobald took up. And it is evident that, by the
time of Theobald's adaptation, *The Duchess of Malfi*
had fallen out of the repertory. The plain and dreadful statement, "she di'd yong", would not be appropriate in the play's new dress.

In recent years we have seen how many close links
there were between the drama before 1642 and the
drama after 1660: the comedy of manners and the
heroic play are seen to have a common ancestor in
the Fletcherian mode of writing. It is perhaps time
we recognised also that the closing of the theatres
closed the tragic account in English drama for 250
years. Though Betterton and Killigrew might revive
Webster and Chapman at the reopening of the
theatres, it was not long before the tragedies suffered
adaptation or neglect. Shakespeare might survive,
but generally diluted and with his more disturbing
characteristics explained away as the stigmata of an
unenlightened age.

It was not until the middle of the nineteenth century that *The Duchess of Malfi* came again to the English stage. It then appeared at Sadler's Wells on 20 November 1850, with Isabella Glyn as the Duchess. But this was no nearer Webster's play than Theobald's version had been. The new adapter was R. H. Horne, the author of *Orion*, who both expurgated and melodramatised. The Duchess was given a name for the first time, and Horne's oddly inappropriate choice was Marina—a name calculated to arouse all the wrong associations for Webster's warm-blooded character. Much of Webster's language was preserved, but was mixed with such Wardour Street stuff as this, the play's opening:

> DEL. [clapping him on the shoulder]. *Good faith,*
> *Antonio—nay, 'twas passing well!*
> *Thou art a prince of horsemen, by my life.*

There was no Julia; the Duchess was strangled off-stage and staggered on to cry "Mercy!" at the moment of death; the madmen of Act IV were heard but not seen. Horne's insensitivity to Webster's genius comes out clearly in his version of

> *I pray-thee looke thou giv'st my little boy*
> *Some sirrop for his cold, and let the girle*
> *Say her prayers, ere she sleepe.*

He turns this into:

> DUCH. *I pray you look to my little boy—*
> *In health—in sickness. Wilt thou?*
> CARI. *Madam! madam!*
> DUCH. *And my poor little girl—beseech thee, let her*
> *Say her prayers, ere she sleep.*

The broken phrases strain towards the pathetic and lose the bare anguish that Webster gave us.

This performance was reviewed in *The Athenæum* for 23 November 1850. The audience, we are told, was "somewhat puzzled by the horror of the situations" but appreciated "the beauties of the dialogue". Both on this occasion and on 7 December 1850, when the printed playbook was noticed, *The Athenæum* expressed doubts on the practice of adaptation:

> We cannot say that experiments like the present are to be commended. While Webster is wholly unfitted for the modern stage,—we have here not even Webster.

It was only, however, in a melodramatic guise that *The Duchess of Malfi* could find its way to the mid-nineteenth-century stage. No more than in Theobald's day was the theatre-audience prepared for the full implications of tragedy.[1]

But in the last fifty years we have come nearer to Webster. There was a William Poel production of *The Duchess of Malfi* in 1892, though even this used a somewhat adapted text. Reviewing the perform-

[1] Horne's adaptation was published in "Tallis's Acting Drama, Part 1", which describes it as "the masterpiece of John Webster . . . lately produced". The adapter's name is not given. Another version of the play appeared in "Cumberland's Acting Plays" (No. 379) about this time. This seems to be an amalgam of Webster, Horne and another adapter: the Sadler's Wells cast-list is given, and the reader is clearly meant to assume that the play is here printed as acted on that occasion. This adapter, however, keeps the name Julia among his dramatis personae. That he worked on the play later than Horne is apparent from his having, like Horne, a two-year lapse after Act I: this was necessary for Horne because he dropped Webster's time-lapse after Act II, and the Duchess's children had to be born: the new adapter pointlessly has both time-lapses.

ance in *Revue d'Art Dramatique*, G. Timmory described Poel as "auteur de l'adaptation", and commented on the strangling of the Duchess off-stage (an interesting reminiscence of Horne) and the sparing of the children, Bosola and Cariola.[1] Apparently the playbill announced the play as being "rearranged for the modern stage".[2] Nevertheless, we can be fairly sure that Poel's production brought back much that Theobald and Horne had rejected. In the twentieth century both *The Duchess of Malfi* and *The White Devil* have been several times acted on the English stage, along with other Jacobean tragedies and dark comedies. *Troilus* and *Timon* are no longer strangers to our theatre, and where they are there is company for Vittoria and the Duchess.

[1] *Revue d'Art Dramatique*, xxix (1893), 144–50.

[2] Cf. review of the production in *The Academy*, 29 October 1892, reprinted in Frederick Wedmore, *On Books and Arts*, 1899, pp. 122–7.

Chapter I

THE WHITE DEVIL

They say many young gentlemen flock to him every day,
and fleet the time carelessly, as they did in the golden world.

THESE are the words of the wrestler Charles
spoken to Oliver in the first scene of *As You
Like It*. The idea of a "golden world" never quite left
Shakespeare. Even in his tragedies we can imagine
a state of things in which disaster could be kept at
bay, or at least a past time in which the sun shone.
Hamlet, we are given to understand, was a congenial
fellow-student, and his early love-exchanges with
Ophelia were as blessed as such things can be. When
Gertrude says:

> *I hop'd thou shouldst have been my Hamlet's wife;*
> *I thought thy bride-bed to have deck'd, sweet maid,*
> *And not have strew'd thy grave* (V. i.)

we are made to feel that the hope was no impossible
one. So too we can imagine Lear before his abdica-
tion day and Macbeth before the witches' greeting:
doubtless Lear was tyrannical before Kent was banished, and Macbeth was ambitious before super-
natural solicitings gave wings to his hopes, yet their
lives before their tragedies began seem compara-
tively sunlit. All through the plays we remember
what things once were, and the evil complexion that
has come upon the world is at the worst only a
recurrent visitation, not a permanent darkness. It is

misfortune, or the force of circumstance, that has brought ill to Hamlet, Lear and Macbeth. This is true to some extent even in *Othello*: though there the characters seem to carry their doom within them, and we can see no path for Desdemona but that which brings her to be strangled in Othello's bed; yet for the characters even of this play things were once good, when Michael Cassio went a-wooing with his friend and saw Desdemona fall in love. But in Webster's *The White Devil* and *The Duchess of Malfi* never has the world been golden. Vittoria could never know or bring peace: we cannot by any stretch of the fancy see her as formerly a gentle girl or in possibility a faithful wife. In this play almost the first words spoken by Brachiano are "Quite lost, *Flamineo*": they would do to describe any of Webster's main characters. The Duchess of Malfi, before her wooing of Antonio in the first scene of her play, has a sense of advancing into dark night:

> *wish me good speed*
> *For I am going into a wildernesse,*
> *Where I shall find nor path, nor friendly clewe*
> *To be my guide—*

and when the wooing is happily done, her woman Cariola sees marks of frenzy in her:

> *Whether the spirit of greatnes, or of woman*
> *Raigne most in her, I know not, but it shewes*
> *A fearefull madnes. I owe her much of pitty.*

Vittoria and the Duchess, Flamineo and Bosola, were not born to the possibility of contented days: we can see them as existing only in darkness, with torches thrust angrily into their faces. Thus when we see one

of Shakespeare's major tragedies, we juxtapose the
darkness of event with the light that could conceiv-
ably be, but in Webster there is no possibility other
than the one presented, there is no world imaginable
but that of the fearful and the mad.

Yet at first sight the ending of *The White Devil*
would seem not so different from that of *Macbeth*.
Malcolm and Macduff enter the castle of Dunsinane,
promising peace and good order to the kingdom of
Scotland, now free from the "dead butcher and his
fiend-like queen". Giovanni,[1] the hopeful prince like
Malcolm, suggests that we learn from the fates of
Vittoria and the rest:

> *Let guilty men remember their blacke deedes,*
> *Do leane on crutches, made of slender reedes.* (V. vi.)

Certainly in the writing of *Macbeth* Shakespeare was
with part of his mind concerned with the evils of
ambition and usurpation: to some extent the play
was a political morality, though it was far more than
that because the world no longer presented the com-
paratively simple problem that Shakespeare studied
in his first historical tetralogy. But *The White Devil* is
in no sense a morality play: not only do we fail to see
Vittoria and her brother as a fearful warning, but
when under the spell of the play we cannot imagine
a world without them: we cannot believe that
Giovanni should inherit his father's dukedom, or that
the surviving son of Antonio and the Duchess of
Malfi should be established in his mother's right. It
is not merely that normality seems tame after the
dark splendours of the storm: that is what we feel in

[1] Or it may be, as Sir Walter Greg has suggested, the English
Ambassador who speaks these lines. Cf. Lucas, i. 288.

Macbeth: rather, there is no road but that which leads to the gallows, where the mandrake breeds.

Yet we can, I think, assume that Webster did not fully realise the significance of his plays. There is a strange gulf between the effect of Jacobean tragic plays on us and the comments on those plays made by the dramatists themselves. Chapman introduced his *The Revenge of Bussy d'Ambois* with a dedication in which he claimed as the properties of tragic drama "material instruction, elegant and sententious excitation to virtue, and deflection from her contrary". Yet *The Revenge of Bussy d'Ambois* is a play in which the hero Clermont is caught up in the mesh of circumstance, knowingly does ill yet believes his fate unavoidable:

> *all things to be done, as here we live,*
> *Are done before all times in th' other life* (V. v.)

is his conclusion. Chapman seems unaware of the conflict between this avowal of predestination and his claim that the play can influence men to virtue. That Webster had little realisation of the effect of his plays is perhaps shown in the indiscriminate praise of his leading contemporaries in the address to the reader which precedes *The White Devil*:

For mine owne part [he says] I have ever truly cherisht my good opinion of other mens worthy Labours, especially of that full and haightned stile of Maister *Chapman*: The labor'd and understanding workes of Maister *Johnson*: The no lesse worthy composures of the both worthily excellent Maister *Beamont*, & Maister *Fletcher*: And lastly (without wrong last to be named) the right happy and copious industry of M. *Shake-speare*, M. *Decker*, & M. *Heywood*, wishing what I write may be read by their light.

When, in 1612, this play was published, there was
hardly a playwright of rank whom Webster did not
include in this catalogue. And could he wish to be
read by the light of Fletcher and Heywood? Was
there any point of contact between *The White Devil*
and *Philaster* or *The Rape of Lucrece*? Yet so little
did the Jacobeans understand themselves that there
is no need to suspect Webster of flattery. He may
well have assumed that his final effect would not be
dissimilar to that of *Macbeth*, that all might profit
from the dread example of Vittoria, that Giovanni
would commence a hopeful reign.

Perhaps this may give us a clue to the strange
extinction of Webster's genius after *The Duchess of
Malfi*. When we pass from his two great tragedies to
the blurred *Devil's Law Case*, the sententious *Appius
and Virginia*, the dreary *Cure for a Cuckold* and *Anything for a Quiet Life*, we must always feel an in-
credulous disappointment. Yet the sudden fall into
insignificance is only a particularised illustration of
the short life of Jacobean tragedy as a whole. Nearly
all the tragic plays of high standing were crowded
into the first dozen years of the century. It happened
that in those years the theatre, poised between a
stiffly ceremonial manner and a later slovenliness,
combined authority of utterance with immediacy of
effect; it happened too that the dramatists' minds
were poised between belief and doubt, preserving a
system of values despite a deep consciousness of evil.
And because their tragedies were not the result of
planned endeavour but rather the fruit appropriate
to that season, the period of high productivity was
short. So, but more obviously and startlingly, Webster's genius sank after *The Duchess of Malfi*. After

33

that, indeed, Heywood and Dekker could furnish the light by which he was to be read.

Because Webster's reputation depends so much on *The White Devil* and *The Duchess of Malfi*, my plan is to devote a chapter each to these plays, glancing at times perhaps at his earlier and later work, and then in the last chapter to try to assess his work as a whole and to trace the decline of his genius. This may provide the effect of a sharp anti-climax, but it will I think help us to determine his true standing as a poet and dramatist.

In *The White Devil* the first character that is introduced to us is Lodovico. He has been banished from Rome, and cries out against the justice of the sentence. But his friends Antonelli and Gasparo remind him that his evil courses have been gross: he has squandered his patrimony and has "acted certain Murders here in Rome, Bloody and full of horror". Lodovico's reply is that still injustice is being done, for others have offended as flagrantly as he and yet go unpunished:

> *I wonder then some great men scape*
> *This banishment, ther's Paulo Giordano Orsini,*
> *The Duke of Brachiano, now lives in Rome,*
> *And by close pandarisme seekes to prostitute*
> *The honour of Vittoria Corombona,*
> *Vittoria, she that might have got my pardon*
> *For one kisse to the Duke.* (I. i.)

And he will, he says, avenge himself on those who have wronged him:

> *Ile make Italian cut-works in their guts*
> *If ever I returne.* (I. i.)

This first scene with Lodovico strikes the keynote for the play. Here is a man given over to evil-doing, who urges that he is no guiltier than the rest, who is not to be taught, not to be consoled, who will go straight on in his path of evil. Essentially he is of Brachiano's kin, and Flamineo's, and Vittoria's, and it is significant that he is concerned in the death of each. It was the upright Macduff who slew Macbeth, the redeeming Henry Tudor who brought Richard Crookback to his end, but in *The White Devil* the fates use Lodovico as their instrument of destruction. The angry and guilty man Lodovico symbolises the absence of order in Webster's universe. In the end it is not those who banished him who feel his dagger, but those who killed Isabella, the woman he pursued "with hot lust". He will come back from banishment avid for bloodshed, and will be quickly diverted from rage against his judges to vengeance for Isabella.

After the note of danger has been struck, we are quickly introduced to the three chief characters of the play—a woman and her lover and her brother. Webster has drawn them with such power, they speak with such authority, that we may not fully recognise the intensity of their evil. We are attracted by them, we give them some measure of sympathy, we realise that they are of our own kin, we shudder and repine at their destruction. But there are here no noble minds overthrown, no conscience-stricken Macbeth. Webster has underlined their devotion to wrongdoing, from which they hardly waver till the moment of dissolution.

First Vittoria, the "White Devil", the "famous Venetian Curtizan" of the play's title-page. When we meet her in I. ii, this description is indeed fitting.

Brachiano's ready whore, she is soon instructing him to murder her husband and his wife. When Cornelia interrupts, Vittoria has one of the moments of panic that come upon her strangely at different points in the play. "Dearest mother heare me" is her first address—odd words for the woman we have just begun to know. Then she attempts a denial of guilt:

> *I do protest if any chast deniall,*
> *If any thing but bloud could have alayed*
> *His long suite to me . . .   (I. ii.)*

This is flat and unconvincing, and contrasts sharply with her later skilful pleading at her trial. Then when Cornelia prays that Vittoria's life shall be short and wretched if she is false to Camillo, Vittoria runs off hastily with the cry "O me accurst!" She behaves in a similar fashion when Brachiano is dead and when her own murderers reveal themselves. There is dramatic skill in thus making Vittoria not always resolute, for we are more likely to believe in her bravery of spirit if at times she cannot maintain it. But her terror at Cornelia's curse gives greater authority to the despairing mother; the implied recognition of her own guilt makes Vittoria's nature more fully apparent to us: here is evil conscious of itself and afflicted momentarily with a great fear. If later in the play Webster makes us admire his white devil, he is here at pains to make us see her as she is.

Her next appearance is in the trial scene, where she is ready-witted and in magnificent control. Abuse is hurled upon her by the Cardinal Monticelso, but always her retorts are skilful, her counter-accusations strong. She addresses the assembled Ambassadors with calm modesty:

36

Humbly thus,
Thus low, to the most worthy and respected
Leigier Embassadors, my modesty
And womanhood I tender; but withall
So intangled in a cursed accusation
That my defence of force like Perseus,
Must personate masculine vertue—To the point!
Find mee but guilty, sever head from body:
Weele part good frindes: I scorne to hould my life
At yours or any mans intreaty, Sir. (III. ii.)

And in her words to Monticelso she speaks with so
great an appearance of frankness that it is difficult
even for us to believe in her guilt:

VIT. *Summe up my faults I pray, and you shall finde,*
That beauty and gay clothes, a merry heart,
And a good stomacke to a feast, are all,
All the poore crimes that you can charge me with:
Infaith my Lord you might go pistoll flyes,
The sport would be more noble.
MON. *Very good.*
VIT. *But take your course, it seemes you have beggerd me first*
And now would faine undo me—I have houses,
Jewels, and a poore remnant of Crusado's,
Would those would make you charitable!
MON. *If the devill*
Did ever take good shape behold his picture.
VIT. *You have one vertue left,*
You will not flatter me.
FRA. *Who brought this letter?*
VIT. *I am not compell'd to tell you.*
MON. *My Lord Duke sent to you a thousand duckets,*
The twelfth of August.

37

JOHN WEBSTER

VIT. *'Twas to keepe your cosen*
From prison, I paid use for't.
MON. *I rather thinke*
'Twas Interest for his lust.
VIT. *Who saies so but your selfe? if you bee my accuser*
Pray cease to be my Judge, come from the Bench,
Give in your evidence 'gainst me, and let these
Be moderators. (III. ii.)

Indeed, when one is seeing the play, one has almost
the feeling that she must be innocent in spite of all,
that somehow we have hitherto misjudged her. We
give Monticelso no credit for the accuracy of his
charges or for dropping the accusation of murder
because the evidence was insufficient. Webster gives
our feelings tongue through a choric use of the English Ambassador: to the French Ambassador's comment "Shee hath lived ill" he replies: "Trew, but the
Cardinals too bitter", and later he exclaims: "Shee
hath a brave spirit." This, making our feeling articu-
late, confirms it, and we are ready to see her as the
victim of oppression. When at the end she is taken
away to the house of convertites, her words of un-
availing protest echo afar off the impotent cry of Lear
against his daughters:[1]

Instruct me some good horse-lech to speak Treason,
For since you cannot take my life for deeds,

---

[1] LEAR. . . . *No, you unnatural hags,*
I will have such revenges on you both
That all the world shall—I will do such things,—
What they are yet I know not,—but they shall be
The terror of the earth. You think I'll weep;
No, I'll not weep:
I have just cause of weeping, but this heart
Shall break into a hundred thousand flaws
Or ere I'll weep. (II. iv.)

38

Take it for wordes—o womans poore revenge
Which dwels but in the tongue—I will not weepe,
No I do scorne to call up one poore teare
To fawne on your injustice—beare me hence,
Unto this house of—what's your mittigating Title?
  MON. *Of convertites.*
  VIT. *It shall not be`a house of convertites—*
My minde shall make it honester to mee
Then the Popes Pallace, and more peaceable
Then thy soule, though thou art a Cardinall—
Know this, and let it somewhat raise your spight,
Through darkeness Diamonds spred their ritchest light.

(III. ii.)

We should note in passing how skilful here is the
mingling of the formalised and the naturalistic styles:
the sudden interruption of "what's your mittigating
Title?" gives an immediacy to the effect which makes
us aware that a living woman with a brave spirit is
to know humiliation. Yet Webster does not allow us
to be completely blinded in this scene. The English
Ambassador is not the only chorus to the play. There
is Flamineo, who for the most part is unusually silent.
He has, however, two brief asides when Monticelso is uttering sentence. Vittoria is told: "you are
confin'd Unto a house of convertites and your
bawd——". Flamineo, startled, says "Who?" And
when Monticelso continues "The *Moore*", he adds:
"O I am a sound man againe." Thus suddenly, and
while Vittoria is still crying out effectively against the
injustice done her, we are reminded of her guilt and
her brother's: there is a kind of squalor in Flamineo's
thus taking the word "bawd" to himself. So we
cannot quite forget what we know.

39

In the house of convertites, when Brachiano
believes her guilty of an intrigue with Francisco, she
affects remorse for all she has done:

What have I gain'd by thee but infamie?
Thou hast stain'd the spotlesse honour of my house,
And frighted thence noble societie:
Like those, which sicke o' th' Palsie, and retaine
Ill-senting foxes 'bout them, are still shun'd
By those of choicer nosthrills. What doe you call this house?
Is this your palace? did not the Judge stile it
A house of penitent whores? who sent mee to it?
Who hath the honour to advance Vittoria
To this incontinent colledge? is 't not you?
Is 't not your high preferment? Go, go brag
How many Ladies you have undone, like mee.
Fare you well Sir; let me heare no more of you.
I had a limbe corrupted to an ulcer,
But I have cut it off: and now Ile go
Weeping to heaven on crutches. For your giftes,
I will returne them all; and I do wish
That I could make you full Executor
To all my sinnes—o that I could tosse my selfe
Into a grave as quickly: for all thou art worth
Ile not shed one teare more;—Ile burst first. (IV. ii.)

The stage direction is given: "*She throwes her selfe
upon a bed.*" This works with Brachiano, but hardly
with us. It is the second time she has said she will
not weep, and the device is now stale. And her readi-
ness to close with Brachiano in I. ii makes it seem a
mere whore's trick when she says "Go, go brag How
many Ladies you have undone, like mee". And in
her final action there is provocation rather than
remorse. She is ready enough to be talked round,

when Brachiano proves penitent and is led to promise her marriage. But our attitude towards Vittoria
here is largely conditioned by Webster's use of
Flamineo as a chorus far more freely than in the trial
scene. There it was only a brief aside that made our
eyes come open: here, while reconciling his sister
and her lover, he is at no pains to overrate the mer-
chandise he traffics in. When Vittoria vows that she
will not continue Brachiano's mistress, his "O, no
othes for gods sake" is weary and amused. And to
each he speaks contemptuously, reserving his grossest
terms for the woman:

> *fie, fie, my Lord.*
> *Women are caught as you take Tortoises,*
> *Shee must bee turn'd on her backe. Sister, by this hand*
> *I am on your side. Come, come, you have wrong'd her.*
> *What a strange credulous man were you, my Lord,*
> *To thinke the Duke of Florence would love her!*
> *Will any Mercer take anothers ware*
> *When once 't is tows'd and sullied? And yet, sister,*
> *How scurvily this frowardnesse becomes you!*
> *Yong Leverets stand not long; and womens anger*
> *Should, like their flight, procure a little sport;*
> *A full crie for a quarter of an hower;*
> *And then bee put to th' dead quat.* (IV. ii.)

When Vittoria lets her rage cool and reproaches
Brachiano with "O yee dissembling men!", Flamineo
will not let her thus impudently put her own fault on
another: "Wee suckt that, sister," he tells her,
"From women's brestes, in our first infancie." And
when Brachiano at length promises that Vittoria shall
be his Duchess, Flamineo's exclamation "Lo you
sister!" taunts at her triumph while sharing in it.

Vittoria does not speak again in the play until
Brachiano's death-scene. There fear comes upon her
terribly. When the dying man speaks of the horror
that waits on princes in their violent ends, her cry is
"I am lost for ever". And her note of lamentation
must be high-pitched, for Brachiano complains:
"How miserable a thing it is to die, 'Mongst women
howling!" Her other speeches here are little more
than exclamations, and when Brachiano's death is
announced by Lodovico, her words are, "O mee!
this place is hell." Thus she leaves the scene very
much in the fashion of her "O me accurst!" after
Cornelia's reproaches in I. ii.

When the last scene of all begins, we read the
stage direction "*Enter Vittoria with a book in her
hand*". Flamineo follows, and begins the scene with
the words, "What are you at your prayers?" Mr.
F. L. Lucas has pointed out that this may well be
an echo from history, for the real-life Vittoria was
on her knees before a crucifix when her murderers,
Lodovico among them, forced their way into her
bedroom.[1] But, if so, this is no haphazard recollec-
tion of a story that Webster had heard or read: his
Vittoria, at her first appearance, was horrified by a
mother's curse. Now, fearing indeed that curse's imminent fulfilment, she turns to the spells of religion
as consolation. When Brachiano lay dying, she urged
her brother to hold the crucifix steadily before him:
"It settles his wild spirits," she said. And now her
book seems to have given her some resolution,
though no piety. Bidding Zanche cry out for help,
she urges upon Flamineo the guilt of suicide and asks
him: "Are you growne an Atheist?" When Flamineo

[1] Lucas, i. 81, 88.

pretends to be dying, his sister treads upon him and
insults over him. She has tricked him, she thinks,
and now she can exult: "You see the Fox comes many
times short home, 'Tis here prov'd true." When her
murderers come at last, she cries for help, and her
"O wee are lost" is another of those exclamations of
despair that punctuate her role in the play. She has
one resource left, her beauty, and that she tries: when
Gasparo refuses her pity, she asks to be killed by
Francisco. That failing, she will woo Lodovico with
flattery:

> *You, my Deathsman!*
> *Me thinkes thou doest not looke horrid enough,*
> *Thou hast too good a face to be a hang-man,*
> *If thou be, doe thy office in right forme;*
> *Fall downe upon thy knees and aske forgivenesse.* (V. vi.)

Hope is gone after that, and she is the stronger for it.
She taunts her murderers, and denies that she will
tremble or look pale with fear. There is an authority
in her last words that has fixed them in every reader's
memory. For the first time there is a genuine expression of remorse: "O my greatest sinne lay in my
blood, Now my blood paies for't"—remorse accom-
panied by a stoical acceptance of the penalty of
action. This remorse, this acceptance are the children,
not of faith, but of dark uncertainty: "My soule, like
to a ship in a blacke storme, Is driven I know not
whither." Finally, at the moment of death, Vittoria
blames her guilt on the corruption of courts:

> *O happy they that never saw the Court,*
> *"Nor ever knew great Man but by report.* (V. vi.)

When we look back on this play, it is the trial
scene and the scene of her death that give greatness

to Vittoria, make us find splendour in the strumpet, the murderess, the woman who, off guard, is a prey to terror. Yet actually in this scene it is only in these brief final speeches that she behaves with authority. But just as Webster used Flamineo's asides in the trial scene to remind us of Vittoria's guilt, so here it is Flamineo who helps materially to establish Vittoria's final impression on us. Now for the first time he speaks of her with respect, and asserts that she is no guiltier, only more famed for guilt, than many another:

> Th'art a noble sister,
> I love thee now; if woeman doe breed man,
> Shee ought to teach him manhood: Fare thee well.
> Know many glorious woemen that are fam'd
> For masculine vertue, have bin vitious,
> Onely a happier silence did betyde them.
> Shee hath no faults, who hath the art to hide them. (V. vi.)

The impression we are left with is of beauty, adroitness, a brave spirit, but Webster would not have us forget that she is the devil of his play's title. From beginning to end of the play there is no gentle impulse shown in her. The dramatist knows that goodness is possible: he shows it in Isabella. But Vittoria is outside the orbit of goodness. She knows what it is, she recognises her own distance from it. It is an imagined, unreachable heaven in the darkness of hell. She is one of the damned, and a source of damnation. Knowing all this, the dramatist does honour to his white devil.

Beside her, the stature of Brachiano shrinks. But Webster has not hesitated to paint him black. First mentioned by Lodovico as a seducer, he describes himself as "Quite lost" in almost his first words in

44

I. ii. When the scene of lechery and plotted murder is interrupted by Cornelia, he is ready to lay the blame on her for what will come:

> *Uncharitable woman, thy rash tongue*
> *Hath rais'd a fearefull and prodigious storme,*
> *Bee thou the cause of all ensuing harme.* (I. ii.)

This trait, indeed, is one of his least amiable characteristics. In II. i he is sentimentally responsive to Giovanni's prattle and ready for a moment to make peace, but almost at once he is brutally rejecting Isabella and letting her take the blame for their separation. Next the Conjuror shows him, in dumb show, the murders of Isabella and Camillo. This scene is crudely managed by Webster, with Brachiano acting almost as a Dr. Watson to evoke by his questions a full account of the Conjuror's skill. There is not the slightest touch of remorse here, but only an infantile curiosity as to how the killing has been done. He swaggers into court when Vittoria is arraigned, but leaves his mistress to the judgment of her enemies, making his exit with a threat for Monticelso but without a word for her. After she has been carried off to the house of convertites, we find him ready to play the hypocrite, affecting grief for Isabella's death: he says to Francisco:

> *Now you and I are friends sir, wee'le shake hands,*
> *In a friends grave, together—a fit place,*
> *Being the embleme of soft peace, t'attone our hatred.*
>
> (III. ii.)

He adds:

> *I will not chase more bloud from that lov'd cheeke,*
> *You have lost too much already, fare-you-well.*

45

Flamineo admires this: "Hee carries it well," he says, but the praise is deadly. After this we feel a kind of pleasure in the way that Francisco tricks him through the letter to Vittoria, and in his submission to Vittoria. For all his ducal arrogance, he is caught by a strumpet's tears, and he has to bear the thinly disguised contempt of the pander, her brother. In V. ii he attempts to re-establish his authority over Flamineo, giving him only a day-to-day reprieve for the murder of Marcello. Yet as he does this, Lodovico is sprinkling the poison on his beaver: the gift of pardon will not be his for long.

His ending is far different from Vittoria's and Flamineo's. The poison sears his brain, and he sees the devil and rats, friends and enemies, capering and threatening. Then he falls quiet as the disguised Lodovico and Gasparo present a crucifix and a hallowed candle and pray over him in the church's Latin. When they are left alone with the dying man and reveal themselves to him, the suddenness of the change strikes sharp upon the nerves. He is too far gone to speak, until summoning all his last forces he cries out *"Vittoria! Vittoria!"* As we watch, it appears that he is to be saved from this last tormenting, that the poison will be allowed to do its work unaided by the murderers' glee. Vittoria and the rest come back into the chamber. But Brachiano cannot speak again, and Gasparo sends them away:

> *What! will you call him againe*
> *To live in treble torments? for charitie,*
> *For Christian charitie, avoid the chamber.* (V. iii.)

In this context the twice-invoked "charitie" is a most dreadful mockery. Brachiano, mute, alone again with

his murderers, is strangled. The overwhelming effect
of this scene comes partly from the thwarted expecta-
tion of relief when Vittoria and the attendants are
sent away for a second time; partly from the sudden
alteration of the friars into Lodovico and Gasparo,
the ministers of the last rites turning into the agents
of damnation, murderers who deny to Brachiano a
sanctified death-bed; and partly too from Brachiano's
crying out for help to Vittoria. Since we know her
for what she is, Brachiano's loneliness must be great
when it is she that he calls upon in extremity. When
he is dead at last, it is apt that Vittoria should say:
"this place is hell."

The scene is terrible but not, in itself, tragic, for
Brachiano has none of the final authority that belongs
inevitably to the tragic figure. He is dragged out
of life ignominiously, like Cariola in *The Duchess of
Malfi*. In his life he proved a tool for a brother and
sister to use as they cut their way to advancement; by
his removal in death the way was prepared for the
revengers' greater prize, the killing of Vittoria.

In many ways the most interesting figure in *The
White Devil* is Flamineo. He is of all men the least
deceived. We have already noted how, by a brief
aside, he brings Vittoria's guilt home to us in the
trial-scene and how, in the house of convertites, he
cheapens the ware he scornfully sells. But as early
as I. ii this frankness appears. The scene begins
tensely, in verse, with first a ceremonial good-night
as Vittoria and Camillo leave their noble guest
Brachiano and then a short interchange between
Brachiano and Flamineo, in which the lover is assured
the lady is won. Then Brachiano relaxes with "Wee
are happie above thought, because 'bove merrit".

JOHN WEBSTER

This is too much for Flamineo, who knows that
merit does not come into the picture. In garrulous
prose he mocks at the show of resistance that
his sister has made:

'bove merit! wee may now talke freely: 'bove merit! what
ist you doubt? her coynesse? thats but the superficies of lust
most women have; yet why should Ladyes blush to heare
that nam'd, which they do not feare to handle? O they are
polliticke, They know our desire is increas'd by the difficultie
of injoying; whereas satiety is a blunt, weary and drowsie
passion—if the buttery hatch at Court stood continually open
their would be nothing so passionat crouding, nor hot suit
after the beverage. (I. ii.)

As the scene progresses, he takes an obstinate delight
in getting rid of the suspicious husband and then
watching the encounter of Brachiano and Vittoria.
It is true that, when Cornelia reproaches her son
with "because we are poore, Shall we be vitious?",
he retorts that his villainy is his sole means to
preferment:

>   Pray what meanes have you
> To keepe me from the gallies, or the gallowes?
> My father prov'd himselfe a Gentleman,
> Sold al's land, and like a fortunate fellow,
> Died ere the money was spent. You brought me up,
> At Padua I confesse, where I protest
> For want of meanes, the University judge me,
> I have bene faine to heele my Tutors stockings
> At least seven yeares: Conspiring with a beard
> Made me a Graduate—then to this Dukes service—
> I visited the Court, whence I return'd
> More courteous, more letcherous by farre,
> But not a suite the richer; and shall I,

48

Having a path so open and so free
To my preferment, still retaine your milke
In my pale forehead? no this face of mine
I'le arme and fortefie with lusty wine,
'Gainst shame and blushing. (I. ii.)

But we cannot mistake the vicarious sensual thrill in his panderism. Flamineo is, of course, a late example of the Machiavellian type, with no Tamburlainian glory about him: he is a remote descendant of the villainous Ateukin in Robert Greene's *James IV*. But above all else he owes much to Iago, who was similarly determined on petty advancement and similarly could not get the act of sex from his mind. Iago speculating on the potentialities of frailty in Desdemona, Iago seeing that Othello's wedding-night is interrupted, Iago putting into Othello's mind sooty imaginings of Cassio in Desdemona's arms: all these bring us to Flamineo holding the door for his sister and Brachiano, and excitedly echoing and applauding the words they speak to each other.

A dramatist is likely to get peculiar pleasure in the drawing of a character like Flamineo: because he is at once the contriver of action, the manipulator of human beings, and also the spectator of action, the appreciative commentator, the man whose thrill may be no less intense for being second-hand—because he is thus a kind of image of the dramatist himself, who contrives and savours at a further remove—the dramatist may well come to identify himself with this character. We have seen how Webster uses Flamineo as a chorus. We remember that Iago is the sharpest-visioned man in the play of *Othello*, and his soliloquised comments on the other characters are almost

alone trustworthy. So, too, Tourneur's Vindice in
The Revenger's Tragedy will play the pander to his
"nest of dukes", will speak the playwright's own
words of hatred, will look upon his contrivances and
find them good. A gentler and baffled cousin of these
figures is Gregers Werle in *The Wild Duck*: he too
is avid for manipulation, for the arousing of emotional
responses in those under his power; and like Flamineo and Iago he is ultimately defeated, aware in the
end that there are limits to his power. Of this company too are the morality Vice, Jonson's Mosca,
Prospero, and the Duke in *Measure for Measure*.

But Iago and Flamineo stand in a special way outside themselves, watching themselves react to the
evolution of circumstance. Just as they derive their
sharpest sensations from the activity of others, so
even those sensations are not so much experienced
as contemplated. Flamineo is all the time playing
with danger—striking Lodovico, braving Brachiano,
killing Marcello—as if he wants to feel an impact
which somehow misses him. After watching Brachiano die, he pretends to let Vittoria and Zanche
shoot him, and plays at being *in extremis*. There
is a stilted extravagance in his words, as he tries to
discover what the ultimate and surely the one truly
effective thrill must be like:

> *O I smell soote,*
> *Most stinking soote, the chimneis a-fire,*
> *My liver's purboil'd like scotch holly-bread;*
> *There's a plumber laying pipes in my guts, it scalds.*
>
> (V. vi.)

Before this, and with the same desire to bring
sensation home, he draws the traverse to behold

Cornelia mourning over Marcello. Her madness does bring feeling to birth in him, but he is not sure what it is, as if the world of direct experience has ever stood barred against him and now he cannot name the sensation it brings:

> *I have a strange thing in mee, to th' which*
> *I cannot give a name, without it bee*
> *Compassion.* (V. iv.)

Still he is observing himself, anxious to classify the experience. It is the nearest he gets to absorption in the moment. When, just after that, Brachiano's ghost appears, he speaks of it as a "terrible vision", yet he cross-examines it truculently, and his "O fatall!" when the ghost throws earth upon him has a mocking air. Flamineo is inquisitive about the universe, as if he cannot quite believe in it. Then he goes off to threaten Vittoria and play his last tricks.

His death is performed in high style, as he demands thunder for his death-knell. He is pleased that he has carried it off well, that there is some goodness in his death, the one thing in his life that he is not compelled to despise. Like Vittoria, he is prepared to put some part of the blame on the corruptive power of great men, but this seems only a momentary weakening. He is in a mist when it comes to a consideration of what follows death: all he knows, all he has, is the existence of his own self in the savage world that he has seen:

> *I doe not looke*
> *Who went before, nor who shall follow mee;*
> *Noe, at my selfe I will begin and end.* (V. vi.)

Because, of all trades, the pander's is the most despised, Webster's triumph in making a tragic figure out of Flamineo is remarkable. He has the privilege of dying after his sister, and his words resound more fully. Though the dramatist was fascinated by Vittoria, Flamineo seems to have come white-hot from his brain. It is in him that we have the most flagrant antinomianism, the strongest scepticism, the relentless and frustrated searching for the meaning of things. In the end he has only his defiance, his truculent demand for the thunder as his universe dies. He has no sense of freedom: his lines have been set down for him: as his blood flows and his voice fails, he rallies his forces and exults that at last he has spoken his words well.

Despite the conventional ending with Giovanni and the Ambassadors, there is little suggestion in this play that the evil figures exist within a framework of good. After death, there is only a mist. Two ghosts are introduced,[1] but the manner of their appearance is significant. In Act IV Monticelso is thinking of his dead sister, is plotting her revenge: he tries to imagine her before him, and then sees her:

> I'le close mine eyes,
> And in a melancholicke thought I'le frame
> Her figure 'fore me. Now I—d' foot how strong
> Imagination workes! how she can frame
> Things which are not! me thinks she stands afore me;
> And by the quicke Idea of my minde,
> Were my skill pregnant, I could draw her picture.

[1] Lord David Cecil in Poets and Story-tellers, 1949, p. 28, remarks that "No plays contain more ghosts and lunatics and massacres than" Webster's. There are no ghosts in The Duchess of Malfi, and the critic here pays an unconscious tribute to Webster's power of suggesting the thinness of the crust on which ordinary life is lived.

Thought, as a subtile Jugler, makes us deeme
Things, supernaturall, which have cause
Common as sickenesse. 'Tis my melancholy—
How cam'st thou by thy death?—how idle am I
To question mine owne idlenesse! . . . did ever
Man dreame awake till now? . . . remove this object—
Out of my braine with't! what have I to do
With tombes, or death-beds, funerals, or teares,
That have to meditate upon revenge?
So now 'tis ended, like an old wives' story. (IV. i.)

When Flamineo sees Brachiano's ghost, it comes just after Cornelia's mad lamentations have affected him more powerfully than any previous experience: he is left alone and meditates on his life corrupted by greatness and the court: to him the ghost appears as the last of a series of horrors, the logical completing term:

Now to my sisters lodging,
And summe up all these horrours; the disgrace
The Prince threw on mee; next the pitious sight
Of my dead brother; and my Mother's dotage;
And last this terrible vision. (V. iv.)

Both ghosts are silent, neither is certainly objective. They testify to nothing certain except to the power of strong imagination. Yet there are hints in the play that the darkness encompassing the life of man is strangely alive. The intervention of Cornelia in I. ii and the consternation she produces, particularly in Vittoria, have a kind of preternatural authority. Her madness in V. iv repeats this effect, so that even Flamineo says: "I would I were from hence." Something similar happens when Brachiano is raving

53

on his death-bed: Flamineo grows superstitious, saying:

> *I doe not like that hee names mee so often,*
> *Especially on's death-bed: 'tis a signe*
> *I shall not live long.* (V. iii.)

Through madness Cornelia and Brachiano seem to become spokesmen for a magical other-world, a world of mists which gather closer around at the moment of death. Men cannot know its constitution or its hierarchies; it can obscurely threaten but makes no promises.

As for the constitution of human society, Webster's intention is not clear. We need to consider both the trial of Vittoria and the election of Monticelso as Pope. First we should remark that Webster is fond of trial-scenes, as indeed are other playwrights of the time. In *Sir Thomas Wyatt*, a collaboration with Dekker and perhaps the earliest extant dramatic work in which Webster had a hand, Lady Jane Grey and her husband Guildford Dudley are brought to trial for their attempted usurpation. This scene has been attributed to Webster,[1] but even if it was not his it may still have been the germ of some of his later writing. Jane in this play is far closer to the Duchess of Malfi than to Vittoria: she is to Guildford "my fair queen of sorrow", and he tells her: "Patience has blanch'd thy soul as white as snow." The trial is unjust and cruel: the lords who

---

[1] Cf. Lucas, iv. 240; *The Elizabethan Stage*, iii. 294. A line from Seneca's *Phaedra*, "Curae leves loquuntur, ingentes stupent", is echoed both in this scene in *Sir Thomas Wyatt* and in *The White Devil*, II. i. 279; but it is freely used by other Elizabethans, including Shakespeare (cf. Lucas, i. 219).

condemn have been more guilty than the gentle resolute children who must prepare for death. Among Webster's later plays there are trial-scenes in *The Devil's Law Case*, in *Appius and Virginia* and in his collaboration with Massinger, *The Fair Maid of the Inn*: in every instance the judgment of the court is at fault, either through false evidence or through corruption in the judge. Virginia is given over as a prey to Appius, and the lying mothers of *The Devil's Law Case* and *The Fair Maid of the Inn* win the verdict they demand. We should notice here a difference from the trial-scenes at or near the end of *The Merchant of Venice*, *All's Well* and *Measure for Measure*, and the ceremonial rejection of Falstaff which concludes 2 *Henry IV*. In the Shakespeare plays justice is in a fashion done. Antonio is saved from Shylock's malignity, Helena reaps her reward, Angelo's villainy is laid bare, the young Henry V makes himself free to win Agincourt. Yet even in these plays of Shakespeare we do not carry from the dispensation of justice a feeling of contentment. We are uneasy about the qualifications of the judge, and his ability to weigh one value or one guilt against another. In Jonson's *Volpone*, indeed, the feeling is much stronger: the court is stupid and ready to fawn on Mosca the new magnifico: we can barely acknowledge its right to mortify a fox. It would, therefore, be a little surprising if Monticelso held our complete respect during the trial of Vittoria. Yet, though he cannot pretend to impartiality and acts as accuser as well as judge, he speaks nothing that is not true. He allows Vittoria to have her way concerning the language in which her accusation shall be phrased, and his final sentence is a model of discretion. The charge of murder is dropped for lack of evidence, Flamineo and Marcello are allowed to go free, Vittoria is sent to the house of convertites after her adultery has been made plain. That she planned Camillo's death is certain to Monticelso, but he does not force the law to proclaim her guilt. Vittoria may cry that he has ravished justice, forced her to do his pleasure, but no charge could be more baseless. She has been lucky in the uprightness of her angry judge. Yet he gets none of our sympathy here: we are too much under the devil's spell. Later, Monticelso is kept apart from the revengers. He forbids Lodovico to pursue revenge in IV. iii, and almost succeeds in dissuading him. Francisco, however, tricks Lodovico into believing that Monticelso, now elected Pope, is playing the hypocrite. There is perhaps a contradiction between Monticelso's behaviour here and his willingness in IV. i to let Francisco see his black book and choose from it instruments of revenge. But, this apart, Monticelso in his more arid way seems to belong with Isabella and Giovanni to the company of the good. His election as Pope is not an irrelevancy, put in to leave fascinated though Protestant Englishmen open-mouthed. It is a suggestion that man, not altogether in vain, strives to bring order into his affairs. Lodovico, whose cry "Banisht!" is the first word in the play, and Brachiano, with his "Quite lost", are outside the scope of the ordered life.

There is a Calvinist strain in Jacobean drama which is commonly overlooked.[1] The tragic writers

---

[1] Cf. Lord David Cecil, *op. cit.*, p. 30: "His theology is Calvinistic. The world as seen by him is, of its nature, incurably corrupt." But what matters most is Webster's apparently unconscious acceptance of the doctrine of election

know little of heaven but much of hell. Webster discriminates clearly between good and evil and, though his characters refer much to the corruptive power of great place, he does not condemn society outright. It is woefully imperfect, but a Cardinal or Pope may do his best to denounce guilt and to discourage revenge. Courts may err and judges grow angry and accuse, but laws may be just and justly exercised. And yet all this seems irrelevant in the face of death and the consciousness of damnation. What comes after life may be uncertain, but there is a terrible certainty in the recognition of evil. That is the portion of Vittoria and Flamineo, and their power to stare it in the face gives them something of nobility. And that is worth ambition, though in hell.

Chapter II

THE DUCHESS OF MALFI

WHEN one turns from the plays of the sixteenth century to Webster's major tragedies, one is always struck by the way the dramatic idiom has approached the manner of non-dramatic speech. Mr. Lucas has noted that when Francisco, seeing Isabella's ghost, cries out:

> *what have I to do*
> *With tombes, or death-beds, funerals, or teares,*
> *That have to meditate upon revenge?* (IV. i.)

we are given "a momentary echo of the style and metrical cadence of the cruder Revenge Tragedy of the earlier Elizabethan stage".[1] If such lines are compared with anything in *The Spanish Tragedy* or even in Marston's early plays, the kinship in style is easily observable. They strike a discordant note in *The White Devil* because they belong to a type of drama that is near the deliberate and purposeful ceremonial. The governing idea of an early Elizabethan play was commonly clear to the dramatist and his audience. A prologue or an induction-speaker would introduce the story and display it as an illustration of a general thesis. Thus in Greene's *James IV* the misanthropic Bohan exhibits the loves and intrigues of the Scottish court to demonstrate the good sense of his own retirement from the public scene; Machiavel, speaking as prologue to *The Jew of Malta*, announces quite

[1] Lucas, i. 238.

simply that the drama will display a man after his own heart; in the induction to *The Spanish Tragedy*, the ghost of Don Andrea and the spirit of Revenge promise that our satisfaction shall come from a simple accomplishment of a revenge-cycle. It is true that in the finer plays of that time there are overtones in the plays' effects and a certain reticence in the dramatists. Marlowe bids his audience applaud as they please the fortunes of Tamburlaine; Kyd shows early signs of a developing interest in the study of a mind under strain; Shakespeare in *Romeo and Juliet* gives us rather more than he promises, rather more than an account of how peace was sadly brought to Verona. Yet it remains true that the plays of the sixteenth century are, in general, illustrations of a set thesis. We are not only clear what the plays are about, we are fairly sure of the kind of attitude the dramatist wishes us to take. But in Jacobean years this clarity and this certainty largely evaporate. That is why so many books can be written about the meaning of *Hamlet*, why indeed so much attention has been given to the study of Shakespeare's characters in his major phase. We are inclined to-day to resent the study of a Shakespeare play as if it were a kind of portrait-gallery, and it is of course true that the total meaning of a play is not the sum of a series of character studies. Nevertheless, in the great decade near the beginning of the seventeenth century the minds of dramatists were directed much more to the exploration of the individual personality than to the enunciation of general truths. We have already seen that the conclusions of *The White Devil* and *The Duchess of Malfi*, with their half-promise of a quieter time to come, are only incidental in the plays' effects.

JOHN WEBSTER

What remains in our minds from *The White Devil*
is a study in certain characters, full-blooded, rash,
and increasingly aware of their doom. I have suggested a Calvinist tinge in the thought of much
of this tragic writing, but it is unlikely that the
dramatists were aware of that. What held their
attention and drove them on was the fascinated con-
templation of the human substance. Inevitably, therefore, their plays do not cultivate the grandiloquent
style of the formal pageant. There may be, as we have
noted, an occasional relapse into a resounding, cere-
monious style; there may be moments of rhetoric
when they are appropriate to a particular character at
a particular crisis, as when Flamineo calls for the
thunder at the instant of his death. But normally the
verse, though its recognisable metrical beat gives
it yet sufficient authority for tragic utterance, has
almost the same degree of flexibility as unpremedi-
tated speech:

> *That's better, she must weare his Jewell lower.*
> > (*The White Devil*, I. ii.)
> *What! will you call him againe*
> *To live in treble torments? for charitie,*
> *For Christian charitie, avoid the chamber.*
> > (*Ibid.*, V. iii.)
> *My soule, like to a ship in a blacke storme,*
> *Is driven I know not whither.* (*Ibid.*, V. vi.)

In each case the shape of the line is not imposed
according to a set plan or in conformity with a set
style; rather, it fits the character in the particular
circumstances of the utterance. And as in Shakespeare's tragedies, so here there is a use of prose which
gives greater range of dramatic style and which is

particularly useful to suggest a state of mind demanding expression with a minimum of formal articulation. This is especially noticeable in Flamineo's part in *The White Devil*—when, for example, in I. ii he speaks of Vittoria in slighting terms after Brachiano has seemed to magnify his success with her, and when in his death-scene his voice rambles weakly on about the lions in the Tower mourning if the sun shines. Flamineo is much given to the rash expenditure of words, as if he is striving all the time for the satisfaction and understanding that come from full expression: when his feelings are not sharply defined, his utterance is, rightly, blurred.

This more naturalistic style of Jacobean tragic writing could not have come about if the actors of the time were not cultivating greater restraint of manner than had earlier been known. The player-scenes in *Hamlet* might well serve as an induction to the whole body of Jacobean tragedy. Speech is now to come trippingly on the tongue: temperance and discretion are to be the player's watchwords. This is not only what Shakespeare and Hamlet wanted, it was to some extent what they were beginning to get. The First Player ventures the hope that the necessary reforms have already been partially achieved. Moreover, we can find other playwrights demanding a natural-seeming manner of performance. In Chapman's *The Widow's Tears*, acted in the early years of the century, Tharsalio doubts the genuineness of Cynthia's grief for her supposedly dead husband:

> *These Grieues that sound so lowd, proue alwaies light,*
> *True sorrow euermore keepes out of sight.* (IV. i.)

And, turning informally to prose, he adds:

This straine of mourning with Sepulcher, like an ouer-doing Actor, affects grossly, and is indeede so farre forc't from the life, that it bewraies it selfe to be altogether artificiall.

The "ouer-doing Actor" was clearly a bug-bear to the dramatist who tried in his writing to preserve the modesty of nature. There is, too, reason to believe that Webster himself wrote the character of "An excellent Actor" that was among those added in the 1615 edition of Overbury's *Characters*.[1] There we find Hamlet's precepts echoed, when we are told that the excellent actor

doth not strive to make nature monstrous, she is often seen in the same Scæne with him, but neither on Stilts nor Crutches; and for his voice, tis not lower then the prompter, nor lowder then the Foile and Target. By his action he fortifies morall precepts with example; for what we see him personate, we thinke truely done before us.

This is close indeed to the words of the final note added by Webster to the text of *The White Devil* when it appeared in 1612:

For the action of the play, twas generally well, and I dare affirme, with the Joint testimony of some of their owne quality, (for the true imitation of life, without striving to make nature a monster) the best that ever became them.

Webster's praise of the acting is notable when we consider his hard words about the audience in his prefatory address, but it is the reference to the manner of the playing that is especially significant.

[1] Cf. above, p. 10.

THE DUCHESS OF MALFI

As we read the plays of the seventeenth century, we must frequently remind ourselves that Flamineo and Bosola were played very differently from, say, Marlowe's Jew two decades before. When we consider the relation of Jacobean tragedy to the twentieth-century stage, we are always—and rightly—inclined to emphasise its rhetoric, its greater range of style, its lack of inhibition. But in Jacobean eyes the playhouse was achieving a new naturalism, an acting-style which was appropriate to the new drama of infirm orientation, the drama that explored and documented but was no straightforward illustration of a given thesis.

We can, I think, see this naturalistic manner developed a good deal further in *The Duchess of Malfi* than in *The White Devil*. The beginning of III. ii will illustrate this. Ferdinand is visiting Malfi, and the Duchess, long since fast-wedded, is ever fearful of discovery. Yet Antonio has come to her at night, as it were in wanton defiance of danger. With Cariola they talk jestingly, intimately, as the Duchess combs her hair and prepares for rest. An edge is given to this clandestine encounter because they and we know that Ferdinand is near. Their conversation is frolicsome, salacious, because of this. They laugh and kiss and mock each other: "When were we so merry?" asks the Duchess, adding "my hair tangles" as she proceeds with her nightly, customary task. There is something almost "fey", certainly irresponsible, in Antonio's behaviour as he and Cariola steal from the room, leaving the Duchess talking and thinking they are still present. What she says then is so informal that the blank verse structure is hardly apparent. As we read it, we must see her combing her hair,

63

punctuating her words with the movement of her arm:

> *Doth not the colour of my haire 'gin to change?*
> *When I waxe gray, I shall have all the Court*
> *Powder their haire, with Arras, to be like me:*
> *You have cause to love me, I entred you into my heart*
> *Before you would vouchsafe to call for the keyes.*
> *We shall one day have my brothers take you napping:*
> *Me thinkes his Presence (being now in Court)*
> *Should make you keepe your owne Bed: but you'll say*
> *Love mixt with feare, is sweetest: I'll assure you*
> *You shall get no more children till my brothers*
> *Consent to be your Ghossips: have you lost your tongue?*
>
> (III. ii.)

At that she turns and sees Ferdinand, who gives her a dagger. Immediately the whole manner of her speech changes: there is authority again in her:

> *'Tis welcome:*
> *For know whether I am doomb'd to live, or die,*
> *I can doe both like a Prince.* (III. ii.)

This kind of dramatic change Webster had used in *The White Devil*, but here the degree of alteration is much greater, the informal style much closer to actuality. There are other scenes in the play where we are made to feel the note of everyday life, albeit of a life lived in the shadow of greatness and of fear. Though the central figure in this play is a Duchess, we see her most often as a private person, with her servants, her lover, her family. Her wooing of Antonio in I. i is quiet and gentle; the scenes of haste and confusion during and after her travail are low-

64

pitched, with Antonio taken by surprise and speaking off guard; the scenes in which Julia, the Cardinal's mistress, appears have all the casualness of tired lust.

The contrasts of tone within *The Duchess of Malfi* inevitably bring into relief the passages of high tension. We have already seen how sharp is the effect when Ferdinand appears with the dagger as the Duchess disentangles her hair. And the long ecstasy of pain in Act IV derives much of its power from our previous intimate contacts with the Duchess. This play works upon the nerves of the audience more skilfully than perhaps any other Jacobean tragedy. Outside the major works of Shakespeare (and perhaps even that customary exception is here unnecessary), the death of the Duchess moves us more deeply than anything else in English drama. For its "great moments", indeed, this play may stand higher than *The White Devil*. Yet we may come to the conclusion that, for all its occasional splendours, *The Duchess of Malfi* gives fair warning of Webster's imminent decline in dramatic power. He has excelled in the moving exploration of the human mind, yet his play is blurred in its total meaning. It is a collection of brilliant scenes, whose statements do not ultimately cohere.

It has been commonly observed, of course, that the play suffers an anticlimax in Act V. When the Duchess at last is dead, and the worn-out Ferdinand, the remorseful Bosola have spoken their necessary words, it is difficult for us to maintain interest in the sequence of events. We have hardly felt Antonio as a character, we know that Ferdinand must go mad, that Bosola will somehow stumble into death: there

is no tension left, no slightest element of doubt. It is
not as if Bosola had the independence of mind of
Flamineo. He accepts the dictate of circumstance too
easily, there is hardly a struggle against fate in him,
he is only an instrument cursed with the gift of consciousness. So, despite the pathos of the echo-scene,
the lycanthropic ravings of Ferdinand, the thorough-
going wantonness of Julia, this last act is an over-
long recession from the play's climax. But this is not
the only structural defect in the play. There are
frequent contradictory statements, sometimes given
in close proximity. When in the first scene Bosola
enters, Antonio thus describes him to Delio:

> *Here comes* Bosola
> *The onely Court-Gall: yet I observe his rayling*
> *Is not for simple love of Piety:*
> *Indeede he rayles at those things which he wants,*
> *Would be as leacherous, covetous, or proud,*
> *Bloody, or envious, as any man,*
> *If he had meanes to be so.* (I. i.)

Yet less than fifty lines later, Antonio adds this:

> *'Tis great pitty*
> *He should be thus neglected—I have heard*
> *He's very valiant: This foule mellancholly*
> *Will poyson all his goodnesse.* (I. i.)

In II. v Ferdinand has received a letter from Bosola,
telling him that the Duchess has given birth to a
child: he raves and threatens, in terms suggestive of
a condition of mind incompatible with patience. But
he will wait, he says, until he knows the identity of
the child's father. The next scene, the first of Act III,
shows us Antonio welcoming Delio back from his

travels and giving him news of his Duchess: "since
you last saw her," he says, "She hath had two
children more, a sonne, and daughter." He adds that
Ferdinand is now come to court and "Doth beare
himselfe right dangerously". But we can hardly
believe in this delay, for Ferdinand is not the man
to smother his rage during two long years. When the
first child is born, Antonio sees at once to the casting
of its horoscope, which threatens *"a violent death"*;
yet this child survives the Duchess and Antonio and
their younger children, as if Webster forgot that he
had originally intended its destruction: in the last
scene of the play it was convenient to bring forward a
representative of youth to suggest that there might
be future peace. In III. i, when Delio asks what
common people say of the Duchess, Antonio's blunt
reply is that "The common-rable, do directly say She
is a Strumpet". This is confirmed later in the scene
when the Duchess, in fear of her brother, asks for
private conference with him "About a scandalous
report, is spread Touching mine honour". Yet immediately after this, when Ferdinand has come to her
bed-chamber, offering her a dagger as an easy means
of death and atonement, she bravely pleads her cause
with him and offers as an argument that "My
reputation Is safe". Ferdinand does not recall what
she told him earlier that same night, but takes
occasion to embroider on the common theme of
reputation's fragility. At the end of III. iii we hear
of a Duke of Malfi, a son that the Duchess had by
her first husband, yet Webster seems to forget this
boy at two later moments in the play. After the death
of the Duchess, Ferdinand speaks of the motives that
impelled his rage against her. Certainly, as we shall

JOHN WEBSTER

see, these motives are not sufficient to explain his
conduct, but Ferdinand would not advance them if
they had not an appearance of rationality. He tells us:

> I had a hope
> (Had she continu'd widow) to have gain'd
> An infinite masse of Treasure by her death:
> And that was the mayne cause. (IV. ii.)

The inconsistency becomes grosser when, at the end
of the play, Delio says the survivors must endeavour
"to establish this yong hopefull Gentleman"—Antonio's son—"In's mothers right". Shakespeare, of
course, was often heedless about the relation of one
part of a play to another, but these passages in *The
Duchess of Malfi* provide an accumulation of structural
flaws. Some of them are incidental, showing nothing
more than the usual Elizabethan indifference to consistency in detail, but Ferdinand's strange patience
during the long interval between Acts II and III is
a more serious matter, throwing a haze of improb-
ability over his character and this part of the action.
Doubtless Webster could not resist introducing
Bosola's immediate discovery of the birth of the first
child, but then proceeded to follow Bandello's story
by keeping the marriage secret for a long period.[1] If
we take this and the minor inconsistencies together,
and add to them the protracted anticlimax of Act V,
it seems evident that, unlike *The White Devil*, this
play was never sufficiently viewed as a whole during
the process of composition.

This, however, comes out on a deeper level in the
tangle of ideas that the play communicates. Are we
to think of the Duchess as an innocent victim, or as

[1] Cf. Lucas, ii. 9.

68

a distant and gentler cousin of Vittoria Corombona, a woman who prepared her own violent end by a rash defiance of the accepted code? The modern spectator will see her, for the most part, as injured innocence, a woman independent enough to disregard her tyrannical brothers' wishes, and to avow her love for Antonio when his lower rank will not allow him to speak first; a woman loyal and affectionate, a responsive companion, a careful mother; a woman not to be broken either by torment or by the approach of death. Seen in this way, the portrait has charm and yet solidity: we can enter fully into the agonies of Act IV because we have grown into the Duchess's friendship, have seen her loving and merry, have seen her directness in the wooing-scene tempered just sufficiently by a touch of shyness. Yet we must recognise that her wooing and her marriage with Antonio constitute an overturning of a social code: she defies the responsibilities of "degree", both as a woman in speaking first and as a Duchess in marrying beneath her. Her crime against "degree" is not so heinous as Macbeth's, but it may be comparable with Lear's. Lear exalted his daughters above his head, gave consent to their usurpation of sovereignty, and divided the kingdom's rule. The Duchess is both over-ambitious in her overtures to Antonio and careless of her Duchy's good.

Moreover, she was a widow, and in the seventeenth century the woman who re-married did not escape criticism. We shall see later [1] that those *Characters* in the 1615 Overbury collection which are very possibly Webster's include a portrait of "A vertuous Widdow" which emphasises the virtue of a

[1] Cf. below, pp. 106–8.

69

continuing fidelity to a dead husband, and another of
"An ordinarie Widdow" which mocks venomously at
the sexual inclinations of a woman unmanned. The
same sentiments appear in Chapman's comedy *The
Widow's Tears*, written about 1606. One of the plots
in this play re-tells the old story of the widow of
Ephesus, with the added complication that it is the
husband who, not being actually dead and wishing
to test the durability of his wife's love, appears as the
soldier and dispels his widow's grief. The other plot
shows how Tharsalio woos the widow Countess
Eudora. Her vows not to marry again had been
strongly put, as we are told by one of her attendants:

'Twere a sinne to suspect her; I haue been witnesse to so
many of her fearfull protestations to our late Lord against
that course; to her infinite oathes imprinted on his lips, and
seal'd in his heart with such imprecations to her bed, if euer
it should receiue a second impression; to her open and often
detestations of that incestuous life (as shee term'd it) of
widdowes marriages; as being but a kinde of lawfull adulterie;
like vsurie, permitted by the law, not approu'd. That to wed
a second, was no better then to cuckold the first: That women
should entertaine wedlock as one bodie, as one life, beyond
which there were no desire, no thought, no repentance from
it, no restitution to it. So as if the conscience of her vowes
should not restraine her, yet the worlds shame to breake such
a constant resolution, should represse any such motion in her.
(II. iii.)

When Tharsalio's suit has prospered, his brother
Lysander expresses amazement at the Countess's
infirmity of purpose. Tharsalio's reply is that the
keeping of vows of constancy is not to be expected
"in these degenerate daies":

70

THE DUCHESS OF MALFI

LYSAND. Mee thinkes yet shame should haue controul'd so
sodaine an appetite.

THAR. Tush, shame doth extinguish lust as oile doth fire,
The bloud once het, shame doth enflame the more,
What they before, by art dissembled most
They act more freely; shame once found is lost;
And to say truth Brother; what shame is due to't? or
what congruence doth it carrie, that a yong Ladie, Gallant,
Vigorous, full of Spirit, and Complexion; her appetite newe
whetted with Nuptiall delights; to be confind to the specula-
tion of a deaths head, or for the losse of a husband, the world
affording flesh enough, make the noone-tide of her yeares,
the sunne-set of her pleasures.

LYS. And yet there haue been such women.

THAR. Of the first stamp perhaps, when the mettal was
purer then in these degenerate daies; of later yeares, much of
that coine hath beene counterfait, and besides so crackt and
worne with vse, that they are growne light, and indeede fit
for nothing, but to be turn'd ouer in play.   (III. i.)

The whole play makes an acid comment on the in-
capacity of love to endure beyond the period of living
contact: it accepts the situation, but does so with contempt. We have indeed a formal exposition of the
current sentiment concerning widowhood in Jeremy
Taylor's *Holy Living*. There, though re-marriage is
said no longer to be held "infamous", as "anciently"
it was, the widow's state is described as one where
the practice of religion and the avoidance of casual
delights are especially appropriate:

RULES FOR WIDOWS, OR VIDUAL CHASTITY

For Widows, the fontinel of whose desires hath been
opened by the former permissions of the marriage-bed, they
must remember,

71

1. That God hath now restrained the former licence, bound up their eyes, and shut up their heart into a narrower compass, and hath given them sorrow to be a bridle to their desires. A widow must be a mourner; and she that is not, cannot so well secure the chastity of her proper state.

2. It is against public honesty to marry another man, so long as she is with child by her former husband: and of the same fame it is in a lesser proportion, to marry within the year of mourning: but anciently it was infamous for her to marry, till by common account the body was dissolved into its first principle of earth.

3. A Widow must restrain her memory and her fancy, not recalling or recounting her former permissions and freer licences with any present delight: for then she opens that sluce which her husbands death and her own sorrow have shut up.

4. A Widow that desires her widowhood should be a state pleasing to God, must spend her time as devoted Virgins should, in fastings, and prayers, and charity.

5. A Widow must forbid her self to use those temporal solaces which in her former estate were innocent, but now are dangerous.[1]

It is against these sentiments that Webster's Duchess goes. A re-marriage for state reasons might have been approvable, but her wooing of Antonio has only the excuse of love.

Webster does indeed go out of his way to emphasise on occasion the rashness and the guilt of her actions. We saw in the previous chapter how in I. i Cariola describes the secret marriage as "A fearful madness" and how the Duchess admits that she is "going into a wildernesse". But at the very opening

[1] Jeremy Taylor, *The Rule and Exercises of Holy Living*, the Nineteenth Edition, 1703, pp. 74-5.

of the play we have a significant passage. Delio
welcomes Antonio back from France, and asks him
for his opinion of the French court. Antonio replies
at length, stating his admiration for what the French
King has recently done, the purging of his court of
flatterers and "infamous persons"—that court

> *which he sweetely termes*
> *His Masters Master-peece (the worke of Heaven)*
> *Considring duely, that a Princes Court*
> *Is like a common Fountaine, whence should flow*
> *Pure silver-droppes in generall: But if't chance*
> *Some curs'd example poyson't neere the head,*
> "*Death, and diseases through the whole land spread.*
>
> (I. i.)

He goes on to add that it is the duty of advisers to
inform the King of "the corruption of the times":
this is not presumption but a noble duty. At once
Bosola and the Cardinal enter, and we see the
dangerous elements in the court of the Duchess.
Antonio's speech cannot have been in the original
version of the play, for its mention of the purging
of the French court has fairly clear reference to the
assassination, apparently at the young King's orders,
of the Maréchal d'Ancre, a man who had grown
perilously great: this event, which was welcomed in
England because the Maréchal's wife had connec-
tions with Spain, took place in April 1617: *The
Duchess of Malfi* must have been acted before December 1614, when William Ostler, who first played
Antonio, died.[1] But if Antonio's speech is a topical
interpolation, inserted for a revival of the play in
1617, it cannot for that reason be dismissed as an

[1] Cf. Lucas, ii. 3-5, 129-30.

irrelevancy. The Duchess's court has indeed its "infamous persons": as soon as Antonio has spoken, Bosola duns the Cardinal for an overdue reward and then describes both him and Ferdinand:

He, and his brother, are like Plum-trees (that grow crooked over standing-pooles) they are rich, and ore-laden with Fruite, but none but Crowes, Pyes, and Catter-pillars feede on them: Could I be one of their flattring Panders, I would hang on their eares like a horse-leach, till I were full, and then droppe off. (I. i.)

And when Bosola himself has gone, Delio adds to our picture of Bosola and the Cardinal:

> I knew this fellow (seaven yeares) in the Gallies,
> For a notorious murther, and 'twas thought
> The Cardinall suborn'd it. (I. i.)

The implication is clear enough: here is a court in need of the drastic treatment that the young Louis XIII had recently dealt out in France. Here, above all, are good counsellors required, not those, like Antonio, who will let the Duchess have her rash will. Webster used the topical illustration to clarify his play. When the added words were spoken in 1617, they must have sharpened the audience's sense that the Duchess, preoccupied with her personal desires, was woefully neglectful of her prescribed duties. We should notice, too, that Antonio at the moment of his death cries: "And let my Sonne, flie the Courts of Princes." This strangely echoes Vittoria's last words:

> O happy they that never saw the Court,
> "Nor ever knew great Man but by report.
> (The White Devil, V. vi.)

We are made to feel that Antonio, like Vittoria, is conscious of wrongdoing and seeks an excuse in the corruptive power of greatness. This is at least suggestive that, consciously or unconsciously, Webster saw the situation of Antonio and the Duchess as not essentially different from that of his main characters in *The White Devil*.

But indeed the more we consider the Duchess, the more hints of guilt seem to appear. There is even a strange parallel between the wooing-scene, where the Duchess hides Cariola behind the arras and then launches into the declaration of her love, and the scene in V. ii where Julia, the rank whore, proclaims her passion for Bosola and then hides him in her cabinet while she extorts a confession of guilt from the Cardinal: in both cases, a woman's frank avowal; in both, a hidden witness; in both, a woman's triumph leading to her destruction. It is difficult to resist the idea that Julia is meant to provide a comment on the behaviour of the Duchess: they are sisters, Webster hints, in their passions and in their consequent actions. There is, too, an independence of mind, a note of challenge, in the Duchess's references to religion. When Cariola has been the witness of her irregular marriage, there is a hint of truculence in her question "What can the Church force more?" And when Antonio replies that a church-service would be a safeguard against the blows of Fortune, she is almost peremptory:

> *How can the Church build faster?*
> *We now are man, and wife, and 'tis the Church*
> *That must but eccho this.* (I. i.)

Later, in III. ii, she follows the suggestion of Bosola

that she shall feign a pilgrimage to Loretto, so that she may escape from her Duchy and join Antonio. Cariola tries to dissuade her: "I do not like this jesting with religion, This faigned Pilgrimage"; but she is told: "Thou art a superstitious foole." In the next scene Cariola's objection is voiced with fury by the Cardinal:

> Doth she make religion her riding hood
> To keepe her from the sun, and tempest? (III. iii.)

And Ferdinand sees in this conduct a sign of complete irreligion:

> That: that damnes her: Me thinkes her fault, and beauty
> Blended together, shew like leaprosie—
> The whiter, the fowler: I make it a question
> Whether her beggerly brats were ever christned.

> (III. iii.)

This is to be joined with the Duchess's cursing in IV. i. She has been shown *"the artificiall figures of Antonio, and his children; appearing as if they were dead"*, and she breaks out:

> I could curse the Starres. . . .
> And those three smyling seasons of the yeere
> Into a Russian winter: nay the world
> To its first Chaos. (IV. i.)

Her provocation has been dreadful, but this longing for the first chaos links her with many characters in Elizabethan and Jacobean drama whose ambitions are thwarted and who would in anger overturn the hierarchies of "degree". When, for example, Northumberland in 2 *Henry IV* hears of his son's death, he desires death for the world:

76

THE DUCHESS OF MALFI

Let heaven kiss earth! now let not nature's hand
Keep the wild flood confin'd! let order die!
And let this world no longer be a stage
To feed contention in a lingering act;
But let one spirit of the first-born Cain
Reign in all bosoms, that, each heart being set
On bloody courses, the rude scene may end
And darkness be the burier of the dead! (I. i.)

We can understand that he should feel like this, with
Hotspur gone; we can understand the cry of the
Duchess. But, just as Shakespeare wished to make
clear the nature and ultimate goal of rebellion, so
here Webster shows us a woman at odds with life
itself. So too her clinging to her own identity as the
one thing, the one value, left in a world gone fantasti-
cally evil—"I am Duchesse of *Malfy* still"—echoes
Flamineo's words near his death: "at my selfe I will
begin and end." There is a grandeur in the egoism,
but its implications are essentially anarchic. In this
connection we may note that in V. ii the charge of
irreligion is extended from the Duchess to Antonio:
the Cardinal alleges that he accounts religion "But
a Schoole-name", whose observances are to be followed only "for fashion of the world". This seems
odd, for nowhere else in the play is there a hint of
such independence of mind in Antonio, but the
comment reflects from the husband to the wife.

Yet despite these links between the Duchess and
Vittoria there is no such easy dichotomy in this play
as in *The White Devil*. We have only to put Ferdin-
and beside Francisco, or the Cardinal here beside
Cardinal Monticelso, to be aware of that. In the
earlier tragedy we saw that Monticelso behaved with

77

some measure of ecclesiastical decorum, especially
after his elevation to the papacy; Francisco was guilty
of the wild justice of revenge, but the loss of Isabella
mitigated his guilt. Here, on the other hand, the
Cardinal and Ferdinand are given over to evil ways:
they curse, threaten, torture, kill, and in the end die
dreadfully. They are such nightmarish figures that in
comparison the Duchess does indeed seem virtue
itself. Moreover, with part of his mind Webster
apparently sees her as innocent. Not only is her very
wantonness gentle and her heterodoxy inspiriting,
but on occasion we have an explicit assertion that her
treatment is not merited. In III. iv, where we have
the dumb-show representing the banishment of the
Duchess and Antonio from Ancona, Webster uses
two Pilgrims to provide a commentary on the action:
they express astonishment that "So great a lady, would
have match'd her selfe Unto so meane a person", but
they add that "the Cardinall beares himselfe much
too cruell" and deny that there is any justice in the
Pope's seizure of the Duchy. And when she is dead,
Bosola sees her as "sacred Innocence" and contrasts
her gentle repose with the dreadful stirrings of a
guilty conscience:

> *Oh, she's gone againe: there the cords of life broake:*
> *Oh sacred Innocence, that sweetely sleepes*
> *On Turtles feathers: whil'st a guilty conscience*
> *Is a blacke Register, wherein is writ*
> *All our good deedes, and bad: a Perspective*
> *That showes us hell.* (IV. ii.)

Indeed, part of Webster's thought in this play is
itself anarchic. In *The White Devil* he could postulate
an ordered world, but saw it as irrelevant to the

THE DUCHESS OF MALFI

damned figures that caught his attention. Here the
postulate has become altogether fainter. The Duchess
is not one born to be damned, yet she goes through
hell. Her revolt against the nature of things seems
justified. The dramatist seems to speak with her
when, before her final parting from Antonio in
III. v, she envies the lower orders of creation because
for them there are no laws to break:

> The Birds, that live i'th field
> On the wilde benefit of Nature, live
> Happier then we; for they may choose their Mates,
> And carroll their sweet pleasures to the Spring.

(III. v.)

In this speech the Duchess re-states more effectively,
more economically, a theme of Marston's in *The
Dutch Courtezan*, which had been written some ten
years before. There the puritanic Malheureux finds
himself enslaved to the strumpet Francischina, and
he enviously contrasts his state with that of "the
free-borne birdes":

> The studious morne with paler cheeke drawes on
> The dayes bold light. harke how the free-borne birdes
> Carroll their unaffected passions,
> Now sing they sonnets, thus they crye, we love.
> O breath of heaven! thus they harmles soules
> Give intertaine to mutuall affects.
> They have no Baudes: no mercenary bedds
> No politike restraints: no artificiall heats
> No faint dissemblings, no custome makes them blush,
> No shame afflicts theire name, O you happy beastes
> In whome an inborne heat is not held sinne,
> How far transcend you wretched, wretched man
> Whom nationall custome, Tyrannous respects

79

JOHN WEBSTER

Of slavish order, fetters, lames his power
Calling that sinne in us, which in all things els
Is natures highest virtue. (O miseri quorum gaudia
crimen habent.) (II. i.)

In *The Dutch Courtezan* we have an attitude of mind
suggested which is much stronger in Webster's play.
In Marston there is a hint of rebellion, but Malheureux is ultimately convinced of his own guilt and
Francischina's worthlessness.[1] In *The Duchess of
Malfi*, however, this cry from the heart is almost
central: it is a touch of eleutheromania, if we may
use Irving Babbitt's term,[2] it shows a weariness of
the demands that the canons of degree might impose.
And with this we must couple a strange remark of
Ferdinand's in Act IV: he has asked the Duchess
"where are your Cubbs?" and then to her question
"Whom?" he replies:

> *Call them your children;*
> *For though our nationall law distinguish Bastards*
> *From true legitimate issue: compassionate nature*
> *Makes them all equall.* (IV. i.)

[1] An envy of the lawless life of birds is frequently expressed in
seventeenth-century drama, even after the Restoration. But in
Rowe's *The Fair Penitent* of 1703, where "tragic" drama has
become reconciled with prevailing morality, the sentiment is given
to the frankly wicked Lothario:

> *By the Joys*
> *Which yet my Soul has uncontroll'd pursu'd,*
> *I wou'd not turn aside from my least Pleasure,*
> *Tho' all thy Force were arm'd to bar my Way;*
> *But like the Birds, great Nature's happy Commoners,*
> *That haunt in Woods, in Meads, and flow'ry Gardens,*
> *Rifle the Sweets, and taste the choicest Fruits,*
> *Yet scorn to ask the Lordly Owners leave.* (II. ii.)

[2] Cf. Irving Babbitt, *The New Laokoon*, 1910, p. 196.

This opposition of law and Nature, with an implication of Nature's greater gentleness, again suggests a
revolt against the fetters put on man. It was an idea
that Webster returned to in *The Devil's Law Case*,
where we read:

> though our Civill Law makes difference
> Tween the base, and the ligitimate; compassionat Nature
> Makes them equall, nay, shee many times preferres them.

(IV. ii.)

And similarly in *A Cure for a Cuckold* young Rochfield exclaims against the rights of primogeniture:
the law, he thinks, is at fault to give all to an elder
brother: though here there is no question of bastardy,
the complaint is essentially that of Edmund in *King
Lear*. Rochfield is treated sympathetically, though
his impoverishment drives him to take a purse. We
can, in fact, see all these utterances as evidence of
Webster's impatience with law and custom, of a
recurrent longing for a "compassionate", undisci-
plined Nature. And so the Duchess does not die, like
Vittoria, in a black storm: she expects heaven, where
she will meet "such excellent company", where the
gates "are not so highly arch'd as Princes pallaces":
at the very least, violent death will "Serve for *Man-
dragora*", to make her sleep.

When, indeed, we come to the fourth act of *The
Duchess of Malfi*, questions of innocence or guilt
seem irrelevant. We have here a long ecstasy of pain
which gives its own cosmic vision. What has led to
the darkness, what may supervene, we do not care.
Moments of torment, like moments of satisfied love,
exist in their own right. Hierarchical conceptions of
the universe, scales of value, no longer obtain. There

is only one good—to remain oneself, to be Duchess
of Malfi still. There is no question of choice: one
must simply be ready to go through with it to the
end. Webster indeed gives to his Duchess a splendour in this act that makes us proud, makes us glory
in the human nature that is ours as well as hers. At
the beginning Ferdinand asks:

> *How doth our sister Dutchesse beare her selfe*
> *In her imprisonment?* (IV. i.)

Bosola replies in terms of deep admiration:

> *Nobly: I'll describe her:*
> *She's sad, as one long us'd to't: and she seemes*
> *Rather to welcome the end of misery*
> *Then shun it: a behaviour so noble,*
> *As gives a majestie to adversitie:*
> *You may discerne the shape of lovelinesse*
> *More perfect, in her teares, then in her smiles;*
> *She will muse foure houres together: and her silence,*
> *(Me thinkes) expresseth more, then if she spake.* (IV. i.)

When she comes, she refuses Bosola's comfort and
Ferdinand gives her a dead man's hand to kiss. We
should note how the horrible is made convincing and
doubly horrible by the simple, everyday words the
Duchess speaks. She thinks it is Ferdinand's hand
she is kissing, and says:

> *You are very cold.*
> *I feare you are not well after your travell.*
>
> (IV. i.)

Then she is made to believe that the statues shown
her are the dead bodies of Antonio and her children,
and when Bosola is driven to say "Now, by my life,

I pitty you", she turns on him with energy and yet
with a mind reeling, no longer surely distinguishing
between the actual and the imaginary:

> *Thou art a foole then,*
> *To wast thy pitty on a thing so wretch'd*
> *As cannot pitty itself: I am full of daggers:*
> *Puffe: let me blow these vipers from me.* (IV. i.)

At this point she curses the stars and bids winter
come for ever. But Bosola points to the invulner-
ability of the stars: "Looke you, the Starres shine
still." It is the completest assertion in Jacobean
drama of man's impotence, of the remoteness, the
impersonality of the cosmic powers. The Duchess
bravely struggles to answer this: "Oh, but you must
remember, my curse hath a great way to goe": but
then she becomes incoherent in her cursing and
leaves the stage begging for a quick death. Bosola
prays Ferdinand to be satisfied with what he has
done, and says he will not visit her again unless disguised. But Ferdinand is busy thinking up new
plagues for her, and his mind runs on madness.

There was a madhouse-scene in *Northward Ho!*,
though it does not appear that Webster's hand has
been traced in it.[1] A group of merry-makers, including a dramatic poet called Bellamont, visit a mad-
house for their diversion: his companions play a trick
on Bellamont by persuading the keeper Fullmoon
that he is mad and must be kept as an inmate: Bellamont resists forcefully, and the jest is voted a good
one. Perhaps this was the germ of the madhouse-
scene in *The Duchess of Malfi*, as the trial of Lady
Jane Grey in *Sir Thomas Wyatt* may have given

[1] Cf. Lucas, iv. 243–4; *The Elizabethan Stage*, iii. 296.

JOHN WEBSTER

Webster the cue for the arraignment of Vittoria.
Like Bellamont, the Duchess is shut up with mad
folk, but for her the ordeal stretches beyond the limits
of the comic. The madmen represent a universe
in which order does not exist: they are the extreme
term in a series to which the other characters in
the play belong. In Act V, indeed, Ferdinand comes
to overt madness, and already he is behaving under
a non-rational impulsion; the Duchess, too, feels her
grasp on sanity grow weak:

> *nothing but noyce, and folly*
> *Can keepe me in my right wits, whereas reason*
> *And silence, make me starke mad.* (IV. ii.)

And later:

> *I am not mad yet, to my cause of sorrow.*
> *Th' heaven ore my head, seemes made of molten brasse,*
> *The earth of flaming sulphure, yet I am not mad.* (IV. ii.)

In Elizabethan and Jacobean drama madness is
commonly used in three ways: as material for
comedy, in *Northward Ho!*, for example, or *The
Changeling*; as a supreme trial through which a man
may pass, as in *Lear*; and as an image of unrelieved
and terrible chaos, as with Cornelia in *The White
Devil* and with the mad folk of this scene in *The
Duchess of Malfi*. A playwright who uses the theme
in this third way can have no easy faith in divine
goodness: there are certain humiliations which not
even the promise of heaven can atone for. And a
consideration of madness raises awkward questions
about human responsibility. The introduction of the
madmen into this play is thus not a mere example
of Jacobean sensationalism: they represent the final

dissolution of an apparently ordered world, and they are fittingly followed by the entry of Bosola in his disguise as an old man, a tomb-maker, a herald of death. When he laments over the Duchess, it is as if death itself were in mourning:

Thou art some great woman sure, for riot begins to sit on thy fore-head (clad in gray haires) twenty yeares sooner, then on a merry milkemaydes. Thou sleep'st worse, then if a mouse should be forc'd to take up her lodging in a cats eare: a little infant, that breedes it's teeth, should it lie with thee, would crie out, as if thou wert the more unquiet bed-fellow.

(IV. ii.)

It is to this that she replies, still with resolution, "I am Duchesse of *Malfy* still", and then she tries to jest with him about the fashions men affect in the making of graves. Her executioners come, with "*a Coffin, Cords, and a Bell*", and Bosola speaks a strange rhyme, on the transiency of greatness, the storms and mists of life and death, the nothingness that is the end:

> *Hearke, now every thing is still—*
> *The Schritch-Owle, and the whistler shrill,*
> *Call upon our Dame, aloud,*
> *And bid her quickly don her shrowd:*
> *Much you had of Land and rent,*
> *Your length in clay's now competent.*
> *A long war disturb'd your minde,*
> *Here your perfect peace is sign'd—*
> *Of what is't fooles make such vaine keeping?*
> *Sin their conception, their birth, weeping:*
> *Their life, a generall mist of error,*
> *Their death, a hideous storme of terror—*

JOHN WEBSTER

Strew your haire, with powders sweete:
Don cleane linnen, bath your feete,
And (the foule feend more to checke)
A crucifixe let blesse your necke,
'Tis now full tide, 'tweene night, and day,
End your groane, and come away. (IV. ii.)

The crucifix, we see, has become an old wives'
charm, a pointless fragment of death's paraphernalia.
This dirge is one with the ravings of the madmen,
but is more terrible because quieter in its summation
of vanities.

At this point Cariola's nerve breaks. She screams
and is forced off the stage. She has been ready to die
with her mistress, but not to endure these living
horrors. The Duchess is near breaking too, but it
shows differently in her. She bids Cariola:

I pray-thee looke thou giv'st my little boy
Some sirrop, for his cold, and let the girle
Say her prayers, ere she sleepe. (IV. ii.)

Yet she has believed the children are dead. Her lapse
of memory would be pathetic, were it not for the
terror that is strongly here. And the greatest terror
of all is that the Duchess, now indeed humanity's
representative in this pageant of death, will not
manage to die well. Yet she recovers, can jest for the
last time about her woman's tongue, and then with
dignity kneels down to die.

The quietness of this is followed by Cariola's
frenzied struggle for life. Now she cannot take
courage from her mistress's example, and she
clutches at one subterfuge after another to postpone
her execution. With her, Bosola has no hesitation,

86

no remorse. "She bites: and scratches", complains her executioner. To Bosola, she is making the fundamental mistake of thinking life valuable. The children are strangled too. Ferdinand's eyes are glutted when he comes on to the stage. He and Bosola are exhausted, like men who have come to the end of a long journey. "Cover her face: Mine eyes dazell: she di'd yong." There is compassion at last, but much more. An old frenzy has gone out of Ferdinand, and for a moment he glimpses his own state, the emptiness of his world now that his sister has gone. Soon a new frenzy will come on him: he will translate his experiences into the blurred shapes of insanity. But for the moment there is no rage, only a desperate wish to recall the past, to find out why it has all come about.

Of Ferdinand's state of mind, of the motivation of his actions, I wish to say something in the next chapter, but first is needed some reference to the character of Bosola. He has a resemblance, of course, to Flamineo: they both speak cynically about other characters in the play, they both affect a kind of melancholy and can address words of scorn to the men whose bidding they do; Flamineo comes to admire Vittoria for the way she dies, and Bosola's final attitude to the Duchess is one of desperate compassion. Clearly they differ in that Bosola determines to avenge the Duchess and to save Antonio if he can. But it would be wrong to regard Bosola as simply a Flamineo who repents. Flamineo, with Vittoria and Brachiano, is set aside from the possibility of repentance: he is simply outside the pale of salvation within which the murdered Isabella and the surviving Giovanni obscurely dwell. He can recognise the

evil in what he does, he can wish that things were
otherwise, but he is not free to change his fate. But
we have seen that Bosola does not exist in a world
where the saved are to be distinguished from the
damned. He is a paler figure than Flamineo, as
the Duchess is paler than Vittoria. The world of
Webster's second tragedy is twilit, where men all
go down at length, in grim equality, to the dust.
All the qualities of this world seem imaged in Bosola:
he is melancholy, envious, unscrupulous, venal,
treacherous; a spy, a torturer; he grows ashamed
of his own shape, and in disguise is first a grave-
maker, then

> *the common Bell-man,*
> *That usually is sent to condemn'd persons*
> *The night before they suffer.* (IV. ii.)

Later he becomes the voice of Ferdinand's conscience, the death-orator of the Duchess, and finally
her avenger. But his revenge goes astray, he kills
Antonio in error and meets his own death haphazardly. He grows increasingly aware of powerless-
ness, saying when he has killed Antonio:

*We are meerely the Starres tennys-balls (strooke, and banded
Which way please them).* (V. iv.)

And among his final words are these:

> *We are only like dead walls, or vaulted graves,*
> *That ruin'd, yeildes no eccho: . . .*
> *Oh this gloomy world,*
> *In what a shadow, or deepe pit of darknesse,*
> *Doth (womanish and fearefull) mankind live!* (V. v.)

Despite all his activity in the play, he is less a character than a chorus. We cannot put his features

THE DUCHESS OF MALFI

together and make a living man out of them. He is simply a creature out of the night, the very dust grown self-conscious, death with a human heart.

That, I think, is the dominant effect of the play, showing us the world as a place where men are madly driven towards death, where the sole value, the one possible human achievement, is a mind unbroken to the end. Yet it is difficult to believe that Webster aimed at this effect, or surely recognised it when the play was done. In quoting Bosola's last words a moment ago, I omitted his self-congratulation on his dying "In so good a quarrell", and the play finishes with Delio's consoling promise that virtue will bring reward:

> "*Integrity of life, is fames best friend,*
> *Which noblely (beyond Death) shall crowne the end.*
>
> (V. v.)

With that he goes to establish Antonio's son in his mother's right. We saw how the play began with Antonio speaking at length on the duties of a prince, on the need for order in a royal palace: Webster comes back to that for his conventional ending: there may be the good discipline in the son's court that was missing in the mother's. But in retrospect we forget the last act, with its punishments meted out, its consolations offered. We forget that the Duchess has neglected the specialty of rule. Only one memory stays fast with us, that of a woman, young, grey-haired, passionate, exhausted, kneeling down to die.

Chapter III

WEBSTER AS A DRAMATIC POET

In *A Cure for a Cuckold*, written about 1625, Webster presents us with a strange piece of motivation. The play opens with the wedding of Bonvile and Annabel, but the first characters we meet are Lessingham and Clare. Lessingham has long loved Clare, though his wooing has been without reward. Now he presses her to be kinder, and she promises to send him a message indicating how he may succeed. When it comes, it reads:

> *Prove all thy friends, finde out the best and nearest,*
> *Kill for my sake that Friend that loves thee dearest.*
>
> (I. i.)

Lessingham, sorely distressed, debates in soliloquy the claims of love and friendship, and then determines to find out if he has, among his acquaintances, a real friend. He announces that he is to fight a duel at Calais and needs a second who will also take part in the combat. Each friend finds some excuse, until he tries Bonvile the bridegroom. Bonvile agrees at once to forsake his bride in the interest of friendship. When they arrive at Calais, Lessingham reveals that it is Bonvile, now proved to be his dearest friend, that he must fight and kill. Bonvile tells him that, in adopting this plan, he has indeed killed his friend and bloodshed is unnecessary. Meanwhile Clare has guessed what has happened, and says aside:

90

> *I fear my self most guilty for the absence*
> *Of the Bridegroom: what our wills will do*
> *With over-rash and headlong peevishness,*
> *To bring our calm discretions to repentance!*
> *Lessingham's mistaken, quite out o'th way*
> *Of my purpose too.* (II. iv.)

Later, when Bonvile's journey to Calais is known, she has this:

> *Oh fool Lessingham,*
> *Thou hast mistook my injunction utterly,*
> *Utterly mistook it.* (III. iii.)

And when Lessingham returns and says he has killed his man, she protests that she meant him to kill her:

> *for I had thought*
> *That I had been the best esteemed friend*
> *You had i'th world.* (IV. ii.)

But then she rejoices that Bonvile is dead, saying that she had loved him and for that reason did not want to live after his wedding to Annabel. But in that case how could she claim to be Lessingham's *"best and nearest"* friend, *"That Friend that loves thee dearest"*, the victim indicated in her message to him? As Mr. Lucas has pointed out, the confusion may be the result of collaboration or revision,[1] but I have drawn attention to it here because it seems a particularly striking example of the blurred motivation frequently encountered in the plays associated with Webster.

Often in his plays the dramatic figures seem to obey neither the impulses of their own characters nor

[1] Lucas, iii. 21–2, 117.

the decrees of fate. They are creatures of a plot which
is to be worked out, and even the plot does not seem
to be thoroughly planned in advance. When we read
The Devil's Law Case, we feel that almost anything
may happen: Contarino and Jolenta are in love, but
Jolenta's mother Leonora and her brother Romelio
wish her to marry Contarino's friend Ercole. The
wooers are both presentable, high-minded young
men, who proceed to fight a duel when Contarino
discovers Ercole's suit. We are given a hint that the
mother Leonora is herself in love with Contarino, but
from all this we could not guess the strange sequence
of the events that actually follow. Here are a few of
them: Romelio tries to kill the already wounded
Contarino, so that Jolenta may inherit the property
he has left her; Romelio persuades Jolenta to pretend
that she is pregnant by Ercole, so that she may
inherit his lands too; Leonora, in revenge for
Romelio's apparent murder of Contarino, tries to
brand him with bastardy and herself with adultery
committed forty years before; there is a final recon-
ciliation of them all, with Romelio marrying a nun
he had seduced, Ercole marrying Jolenta (who no
longer loves Contarino), and Contarino (who apparently no longer loves Jolenta) marrying the sixty-
year-old Leonora. Now if Webster were presenting
all this with a Jonsonian detachment, indicating with
a lift of the eyebrows the incomprehensibilities of
human action—if there were expressed or implied
anywhere in the play a hint of puzzlement, a comment on the strangeness of it all—then indeed the
playwright's attitude might be clear and acceptable.
But Webster gives no such hint or comment.
Romelio is a cynical villain, who in the end "Most

willingly" marries his ex-nun Angiolella. Leonora,
unscrupulous, lecherous, finally gets the young Contarino, whose last words are: "And to you deare
Lady, I have entirely vowed my life." Ariosto the
judge ends the play thus:

> *so we leave you,*
> *Wishing your future life may make good use*
> *Of these events, since that these passages,*
> *Which threatned ruine, built on rotten ground,*
> *Are with successe beyond our wishes crown'd.* (V. v.)

If this means anything, it is that everyone has had a
narrow escape and must not run such risks again.

Elsewhere, too, we find the behaviour of characters controlled by the demands of a particular
moment in the play. At times indeed the departure
from consistency becomes as flagrant as it often is in
Fletcher. In *Appius and Virginia*, Appius is presented
as a lustful hypocrite, an unjust judge, a starver of
soldiers, yet in the end he is made to die resolutely
and to win praise from the wronged Virginius: he
showed, we are told, "a noble strain" and "dy'd like
a Roman Gentleman". This is dramatically effective,
for it enables Webster to contrast the deaths of
Appius and his follower Clodius, as in *The Duchess
of Malfi* he had contrasted the deaths of the Duchess
and Cariola. But no violence is done to our previous
conception of the Duchess and Cariola by the ways
in which they die: along with the intense dramatic
shock, we recognise an appropriateness, an inevit-
ability. But in Appius there is no previous hint that
he will die bravely. Just as in *A King and No King*
Arbaces changes in Act V into a satisfactory Prince
Consort, and in *The Maid's Tragedy* Evadne grows

JOHN WEBSTER

repentant and anxious to avenge her dishonour, so here we feel that Webster has aimed merely at the effective moment. Similarly he makes Virginius weaken and almost decide to let Appius live, so that the dead body of Virginia may be brought on the stage and definitively harden her father's heart: the Virginius who had killed his daughter rather than let her fall into the hands of Appius would not have been likely to stay the executioner's hand. And after the same fashion Webster introduces a last-act quarrel between Virginius and Icilius, Virginia's betrothed: Icilius has to be persuaded that the killing of Virginia was justified and not "unnatural and damnable": the storm is soon over, and they are allies again. The incident is a mere distraction, like the more elaborate quarrel and reconcilement of Amintor and Melantius in *The Maid's Tragedy*. There has been much disputing concerning the date of *Appius and Virginia*,[1] but this sacrifice of coherence in action and character for the sake of a momentarily increased tension is surely evidence that the play came after and not before the two major tragedies.

The same sort of thing is apparent in the two other plays in which Webster's hand has been traced near the end of his career. Thus in *Anything for a Quiet Life*, which he shared with Middleton, Lady Cressingham is presented for practically the whole of the play as the heartless young wife of an old and doting husband. She makes him sell his land, disinherit his eldest son, send his younger children to be boarded with a London citizen, and finally reduces him to living on an allowance from her. At her penultimate

[1] Cf. above, p. 7; Sir Edmund Chambers, *The Elizabethan Stage*, iii. 508–9, dates the play *c.* 1608.

94

appearance in the play she laughs at Young Cressingham's warning that she will surely be punished for
her ill deeds. "Oh! shee is lost to any kinde of goodness," he says. Yet a few pages later she enters *"in
civil habit"*, no longer in the rash finery that she has
hitherto worn, and announces that her outrageous
conduct has been intended simply to cure her old
husband of his addiction to gambling and alchemy:
he was bankrupting himself by those vices, and now
she has destroyed his alchemical apparatus and
taught him an inclusive lesson.

But perhaps the most puzzling case of all is provided by *The Fair Maid of the Inn*, which was published as Fletcher's but has been assigned to Webster,
Massinger and Ford by H. Dugdale Sykes.[1] As in
The Devil's Law Case, a mother tries to prove her son
illegitimate: in this instance, the reason is simply that
she fears for his life because of a quarrel between
their family and another. This is thin indeed, but is
not the strangest piece of motivation in the play.
That is to be found in the relations between Cesario,
his sister Clarissa, and Biancha, the fair maid of the
inn. The play opens with Cesario, like Laertes, advis-
ing his sister not to be over-free with her favours. His
first words are:

> *Interpret not* Clarissa, *my true zeale*
> *In giving you councell, to transcend the bounds*
> *That should confine a brother.* (I. i.)

He loves her, he says, "With more than common
ardour." He gives her a ring which she must not part
with until she is sure that her choice of husband is

---

[1] Cf. above, p. 8.

the right one and until she has made that choice
known to her brother. As a token of agreement she
gives him her hand, "Which," he says, "were it not
my sisters, I should kisse With too much heate."
There is in fact in this first scene every indication of
a barely suppressed incestuous passion. Cesario is
enraged to find the ring on his friend Mentivole's
finger, and these are the terms that he then addresses
to Clarissa:

> Then shall I ever hate thee, oh thou false one;
> Hast thou a Faith to give unto a friend,
> And breake it to a brother? did I not
> By all the tyes of blood importune thee
> Never to part with it without my knowledge?
> Thou might'st have given it to a Muliter,
> And made a contract with him in a stable
> At as cheap a price of my vengeance: never more
> Shall a Womans trust beguile me; You are all
> Like Reliques: you may well be look't upon,
> But come a man to'th handling of you once,
> You fall in peeces.   (II. iv.)

When Mariana, his mother, urges him to travel
because of the dangerous enmity between him and
Mentivole, he refuses because, he thinks, Mentivole
would seize the opportunity of his absence to marry
Clarissa. When, after this, Mariana claims that he is
not really her son but a child that she pretended was
hers in order to please her husband, the Duke is so
struck by the young man's nobility of bearing that
he orders Mariana to marry him or to give him three-
quarters of her estate. Cesario urges his mother to
the match, and when she refuses suggests marriage

WEBSTER AS A DRAMATIC POET

with Clarissa: it was only because of their assumed
relationship, he says, that

> *no loose*
> *No wanton heat of youth, desir'd to claime*
> *Priority in thy affections, other*
> *Then nature might commend.* (IV. i.)

But Clarissa's obduracy defeats this project too, and
he turns again to Biancha, the fair maid of the inn
who is of course really of noble lineage. In I. i he told
Clarissa of his love for Biancha, assuring her that it
was as virtuous as the maid herself was. Yet in III. i
we find him attempting to seduce her: she will listen,
however, only to a marriage-proposal. Then in IV. i
Biancha, having heard that he is no longer a noble-
man's son, says she is now ready for the marriage
which previously the disparity in their conditions
prevented. For the moment he has higher game in
view, and sends her away with a contemptuous kiss.
But when Mariana and Clarissa both reject his
advances, he goes again to the inn and would marry
Biancha post-haste: now she will have none of him,
as his last refusal made her vow to live a single life.
In the last act the Duke urges that the now ladified
Biancha shall marry Cesario: he rejoices, and her
comment is "Kneele not, all forgiven". It may well
be that these odd twists of inclination in Cesario,
these inconsistencies in the behaviour of both Cesario
and Biancha, may be due to the collaborative method
used in the writing of the play. Indeed, no single
dramatist in a waking state could contradict himself so often and so flatly. Yet the three writers who
were probably concerned acquiesced in this mode of
composition, knowing full well that it must lead

97

to inconsistencies of behaviour, an inadequacy of motive, a stress on the scene-unit and on the momentary dramatic effect. About 1625, then, when this play was written, Webster could be more or less indifferent to the preservation of a motive-pattern. Any motive could be taken up and quickly dropped. He and his collaborators did not ask themselves or each other awkward questions about the manner of men and women they were presenting. Clare in *A Cure for a Cuckold*, Romelio in *The Devil's Law Case*, Appius in *Appius and Virginia*, Lady Cressingham in *Anything for a Quiet Life*, Cesario in *The Fair Maid of the Inn*: all were, to a greater or lesser degree, not human portraits but actors' parts.

If we turn back to *The White Devil* and *The Duchess of Malfi*, we find of course a great difference. Here Webster, in dedication and prefatory address, makes it clear that he is engaged in a serious task; here there is consistency of behaviour in the major figures, as we can see at a glance by comparing the deaths of Vittoria and the Duchess and noting how each is appropriate to the woman who suffers it. We have seen a minor inconsistency in Monticelso's giving his black book to Francisco and then trying to dissuade Lodovico from the accomplishment of revenge. We have seen Bosola experiencing a change of heart, yet the character remained all of a piece, a coherent emblem of the Malfi world. Yet we have seen too that, in its structural defects and in the unresolved contradictions of its thought, *The Duchess of Malfi* does anticipate the later plays. Indeed, it would be surprising if it did not. According to Mr. Lucas's dates,[1] five years separate *The Duchess* from

[1] Lucas, i. 54.

Webster's next surviving play, *The Devil's Law Case*: the only intervening dramatic work seems to be *The Guise*, which is lost. But the dramatic style of Webster's decline was not likely to come altogether unheralded. Just as *Timon of Athens*, despite its kinship with *Lear*, anticipates Shakespeare's final romances in its black-and-white characterisation, its relentless treatment of even minor evil-doers,[1] so *The Duchess of Malfi* in one important instance anticipates Webster's later handling of dramatic character. This is in the figure of Ferdinand, Duke of Calabria, brother of the Duchess of Malfi, murderer, madman and (I think) lover.

Not that we find strange variations in Ferdinand's conduct, as we do with Appius dying nobly after an infamous career, Lady Cressingham revealing a virtuous intent hitherto well concealed, or Cesario transferring his affections haphazardly between his sister and the fair maid of the inn: rather, Ferdinand is puzzling in the way that Clare is puzzling in *A Cure for a Cuckold* or Cesario in his attitude towards Clarissa. We do not understand why Clare bade Lessingham kill his dearest friend, we are not sure whether or not Cesario is conscious of an incestuous inclination. We are similarly in the dark concerning Ferdinand's motives in the persecution of the Duchess. We should note, indeed, that Webster puts the whole weight of the persecution on him. Certainly in I. i the Cardinal joins him in forbidding their sister to marry again, it is the Cardinal who procures her banishment from Ancona, and it is

[1] In *Shakespeare's Tragedies and Other Studies in Seventeenth Century Drama*, 1950, pp. 113–24, I have tried to establish this connection between *Timon* and the romances.

made abundantly clear that the Cardinal is privy to her death. But when the two men appear together there is no question which is the more deeply moved: in I. i the Cardinal is content with general comment on the frailty of widows, but Ferdinand's words are as gross, as full of thwarted passion, as Iago's in the first scene of Othello: he threatens the Duchess with his father's poniard in a speech where the phallic implications are not disguised:

> *You are my sister,*
> *This was my Fathers poyniard: doe you see,*
> *I'll'd be loth to see't looke rusty, 'cause 'twas his:*
> *I would have you to give ore these chargeable Revels;*
> *A Vizor, and a Masque are whispering roomes*
> *That were nev'r built for goodnesse: fare ye well:*
> *And woemen like that part, which (like the Lamprey)*
> *Hath nev'r a bone in't.* (I. i.)

It is Ferdinand who controls the slow tormenting and execution in Act IV. It is Ferdinand who suffers lycanthropy when his sister is dead. If the action of the play is to be comprehensible, we must assume in Ferdinand an incestuous passion of which he is not fully aware. After his sister is dead, he tries indeed to examine his own motives:

> *For let me but examine well the cause;*
> *What was the meanenes of her match to me?*
> *Onely I must confesse, I had a hope*
> *(Had she continu'd widow) to have gain'd*
> *An infinite masse of Treasure by her death:*
> *And that was the mayne cause; her Marriage—*
> *That drew a streame of gall quite through my heart.*
> (IV. ii.)

We saw in the previous chapter that Ferdinand's hope to gain an infinite mass of treasure was inconsistent with the reference in the play to the Duchess's son by her first husband: either, then, Webster wished here to emphasise Ferdinand's uncertainty about his own motives, or the dramatist was himself not fully conscious of the springs of action in his play. If this second theory seems fanciful, we can remind ourselves again of Clare's never properly explained message to Lessingham in *A Cure for a Cuckold*. But, whether or not Webster knew it, he drew Ferdinand as a man who could not rid himself of his sister's image. When in II. v he has learned that a child has been born to the Duchess, his mind conjures up frenzied pictures of her lust, while the Cardinal rebukes him for his "intemperate anger". When she has become his prisoner, Bosola taunts him with the suggestion that her mind yet dwells on the pleasures of her marriage:

> *this restraint*
> *(Like English Mastiffes, that grow feirce with tying)*
> *Makes her too passionately apprehend*
> *Those pleasures she's kept from.* (IV. i.)

From this Ferdinand turns in horror:

> *Curse upon her!*
> *I will no longer study in the booke*
> *Of anothers heart.* (IV. i.)

Saying "informe her what I told you", he leaves the stage as the Duchess enters. When he comes into her presence, it is in darkness and with a dead man's hand thrust between them: the mad symbolism needs no underlining. At the end of the scene he is again

alone with Bosola, who in asking mercy for the
Duchess uses terms that make Ferdinand's passion
flame more dreadfully:

'Faith, end here:
And go no farther in your cruelty—
Send her a penetentiall garment, to put on,
Next to her delicate skinne, and furnish her
With beades, and prayer bookes. (IV. i.)

The mention of "her delicate skinne" brings this
from Ferdinand:

Damne her, that body of hers,
While that my blood ran pure in't, was more worth
Then that which thou wouldst comfort, (call'd a soule).
(IV. i).

He does not appear again until the Duchess is dead.
Then he speaks like a man exhausted, and his famous
words "Cover her face: Mine eyes dazell: she di'd
yong," are the utterance of one whose passion is
spent. Vindice in *The Revenger's Tragedy* finds in
murder a substitute for his mistress's love. So here
Ferdinand is momentarily free from his consuming
rage, he can feel pity and remind himself that he and
his sister were twins. Very soon he is to experience
a wild remorse, but for an instant memory brings
back a gentle affection. That memory becomes in-
tolerable, and from then until his death he is to see
himself as a wolf. His sanity returns with his final
words in the play:

My sister, oh! my sister, there's the cause on't.
"Whether we fall by ambition, blood, or lust,
"Like Diamonds, we are cut with our owne dust. (V. v.)

The last two lines form a sententious generalisation'
and perhaps we should not attach too much import-
ance to the rhyming of "dust" and "lust", but we
cannot overlook the anguish of lost affection in "My
sister, oh! my sister".

When one goes through the play in this fashion,
isolating the part of Ferdinand and weighing his
speeches, there seems only one explanation of his
conduct. There is no "motiveless malgnity" here, as
is plain if we compare him with Lorenzo in *The
Spanish Tragedy*. Kyd wanted a villain for his play,
and Lorenzo was a man who could hang or stab with
a shrug. At the end he must be despatched, but there
is no long agony for him, no ungovernable rage
before the commission of crime or remorse after it.
Ferdinand is not a casual and convenient villain but
a tragic figure. Yet, we must ask, if Ferdinand is
tragic, why does he not more successfully carry the
burden of Act V? Shakespeare's *Antony and Cleopatra*
ends in tragic splendour, though Antony dies in the
fourth act. Cleopatra by herself can sustain the tragic
theme, but the virtue has gone out of Ferdinand and
Webster's play ends in tedium.

One might partially explain this by pointing to the
element of strain in Ferdinand's ravings. Webster
could draw madness powerfully, as he did with Cornelia in *The White Devil*; he could heart-rendingly
show us the Duchess crossing for a moment into
the borderland of the mind's darkness; yet the
lycanthropy of Ferdinand is mere rage and bluster.
He has none of that quality of vision that preserves
the stature of the mad Lear or of Hieronimo in the
interpolated painter's scene in *The Spanish Tragedy*;
until his last moment he shows no awareness of his

own condition. In this last act, indeed, he is not
tragic but sub-human, beyond the reach of our sympathy because his thought-processes never for an
instant come near ours. It is difficult but not impossible to have a tragic figure with restricted powers
of understanding: Shakespeare contrived this in
Othello, but he was careful to preserve the character's impressiveness of demeanour. Ferdinand in
Act V has no understanding, no dignity: he has
become only a horrible illustration of the effects of
crime. In fact, Ferdinand is not even the central
figure of the last act: Antonio, Bosola, the Cardinal,
Julia are given at least equal prominence with him.

We are driven to the conclusion that Webster was
not aware of the potentialities of this character, and
that strengthens our doubt concerning the motivation of Ferdinand's conduct. Are we to assume that
Webster, needing a villain, did not at first consider
too curiously why Ferdinand should be strongly
opposed to the re-marriage of the Duchess? Certainly
the Cardinal is given no motive. But from the beginning Ferdinand takes the lead, and perhaps almost
insensibly Webster was led to suggest in him the
one set of feelings that could adequately explain his
violence. It is notable that Bosola, though he speaks
words that provoke Ferdinand's passion, never
overtly comments on his attitude towards his sister.
Yet Bosola is often Webster's chorus, and the oppor-
tunities for comment were many. It is as if the matter
remained blurred in Webster's mind, as the behaviour of so many later characters apparently did.

Thus *The Duchess of Malfi* appears defective not
only in its general structure, in the consistency of its
details, in the coherence of its underlying thought,

but in the conception of a major character. It remains, of course, for its best scenes near the peak of Jacobean achievement, but we should not neglect the implications of its shortcomings. We are made to realise not only how much in the dark a great dramatist can work but how necessary for complete success is a firm grasp of characterisation. This grasp Webster had in *The White Devil*. Vittoria, Flamineo and Brachiano are figures whose inner coherence becomes clearer as we examine them more deeply. Even, for example, Flamineo's fantastic trickery with the pistols in the final act, his bizarre pretence of death, are logically consequent on his reaction to Cornelia's madness and Brachiano's ghost: he is goading himself, as it were, into sensation, straining after the feelings that he cannot quite reach. And the Duchess of Malfi herself is drawn with the same sure hand, as is the dim, fluctuating shadow called Bosola. But Ferdinand leaves us perplexed, not quite certain of the dramatist's purpose. We have seen it possible to dig from the play the elements of his character and bring them into coherence, but even then we have a sense of potentialities imperfectly realised. We are reminded once again of the hand of Fletcher, the dramatist who manipulated even his main characters according to the requirements of the individual scene. The old way of regarding an Elizabethan play as a gallery of character-portraits was wrong in that it rested often on the kind of excavation work we have done with Ferdinand here: we must try always to see a dramatic character as it appears within the context of the whole play. But if that is remembered, characterisation remains an important concern of the critic of Shakespeare or Webster or any other tragic dramatist. The action of a tragedy has a cosmic significance, it symbolises the general condition of humanity. But it will not make an impact upon us unless the playwright's chief characters are acceptable representatives of our own kind. They may be highly complex, puzzling at first, but we must feel that the playwright knows what he is about. When the character is amorphous, insufficiently thought out, it cannot effectively act as the medium through which the dramatist's vision of the universe is conveyed to us. And in *The Duchess of Malfi* Ferdinand's part in the action constitutes him a major character.

But if in characterisation Webster's grasp is uncertain except in *The White Devil*, we can I think find inequalities of style in every one of his plays. This perhaps can be seen most clearly if we turn first to his non-dramatic work, especially to the thirty-two "characters" added to the sixth edition of the Overbury collection, published in 1615, and to the elegy on Prince Henry, called *A Monumental Column* and written immediately after the Prince's death in 1612. The prose of the characters is tough and sinewy, with much play with antithesis and classical allusion. The matter is generally satiric and, when occasion is, bawdy. "An ordinarie Widdow", "A Distaster of the Time", "A Roaring Boy", "An Intruder into favour", "A Button-maker of Amsterdame" are some of the titles which give the writer grounds for castigation. But sometimes his theme is praise, as in this character of "A vertuous Widdow":

Is the Palme-tree, that thrives not after the supplanting of her husband. For her Childrens sake she first marries, for she married that she might have children, and for their sakes she marries no more. She is like the purest gold, only imploid for Princes meddals, she never receives but one mans impression; the large jointure moves her not, titles of honour cannot sway her. To change her name were, shee thinkes, to commit a sin should make her asham'd of her husbands Calling: shee thinkes shee hath traveld all the world in one man; the rest of her time therefore shee directs to heaven. Her maine superstition is, shee thinkes her husbands ghost would walke should shee not performe his Will: shee would doe it, were there no Prerogative Court. Shee gives much to pious uses, without any hope to merit by them: and as one Diamond fashions another; so is shee wrought into workes of Charity, with the dust of ashes of her husband. Shee lives to see her selfe full of time, being so necessary for earth, God calles her not to heaven, till she bee very aged: and even then, though her naturall strength faile her, shee stands like an ancient *Piramid*; which the lesse it growes to mans eye, the nearer it reaches to heaven: this latter Chastity of Hers, is more grave and reverend, then that ere shee was married; for in it is neither hope, nor longing, nor feare, nor jealousie. Shee ought to bee a mirrour for our yongest Dames, to dresse themselves by, when shee is fullest of wrinkles. No calamity can now come neere her, for in suffering the losse of her husband, shee accounts all the rest trifles: shee hath laid his dead body in the worthyest monument that can be: Shee hath buried it in her owne heart. To conclude, shee is a Relique, that without any superstition in the world, though she will not be kist, yet may be reverenc't.

If this is Webster's, we should do well to remember it as a gloss on *The Duchess of Malfi*.[1] Indeed it is heavily sententious and on the side of conventional thought. It does, I think, strengthen our view that,

[1] Cf. above, pp. 69–70.

on the surface of Webster's mind, *The Duchess of
Malfi* was a warning to the rash and the wanton. His
sympathy with the Duchess, his intuitive understanding of the conduct appropriate to her, welled up
from deeper levels than were touched by these "characters". As a necessity of the character-form, the
portraits are built up in a series of commonplaces or
comparisons, just as in this speech of Monticelso
during the arraignment of Vittoria:

> *Shall I expound whore to you? sure I shal;*
> *Ile give their perfect character. They are first,*
> *Sweete meates which rot the eater: In mans nostrill*
> *Poison'd perfumes. They are coosning Alcumy,*
> *Shipwrackes in Calmest weather. What are whores?*
> *Cold Russian winters, that appeare so barren,*
> *As if that nature had forgot the spring.*
> *They are the trew matteriall fier of hell,*
> *Worse then those tributes ith low countries payed,*
> *Exactions upon meat, drinke, garments, sleepe,*
> *I even on mans perdition, his sin.*
> *They are those brittle evidences of law*
> *Which forfait all a wretched mans estate*
> *For leaving out one sillable. What are whores?*
> *They are those flattering bels have all one tune*
> *At weddings, and at funerals: your ritch whores*
> *Are only treasuries by extortion fild,*
> *And emptied by curs'd riot. They are worse,*
> *Worse then dead bodies, which are beg'd at gallowes*
> *And wrought upon by surgeons, to teach man*
> *Wherin hee is imperfect.   Whats a whore?*
> *Shees like the guilty conterfetted coine*
> *Which who so eare first stampes it, brings in trouble*
> *All that receave it.   (III. ii.)*

Here we have blank verse, and a dramatic point is made by the repetition of "What are whores?" But in other respects the speech resembles the "character" closely. The action of the play stands still while the writer builds up his set-piece. We can admire the ingenuity of the figures, and at the same time feel that the playwright's schoolmasterly sentiments are his own rather than Monticelso's. We have something similar in the first scene of *The Duchess of Malfi*, where Delio has commented that the Cardinal is said to be "a brave fellow" who has gambled, courted ladies and fought single combats. Antonio replies:

Some such flashes superficially hang on him, for forme: but observe his inward Character: he is a mellancholly Churchman: The Spring in his face, is nothing but the Ingendring of Toades: where he is jealious of any man, he laies worse plots for them, than ever was impos'd on *Hercules*: for he strewes in his way Flatterers, Panders, Intelligencers, Atheists, and a thousand such politicall Monsters: he should have been Pope: but instead of comming to it by the primative decensie of the church, he did bestow bribes, so largely, and so impudently, as if he would have carried it away without heavens knowledge.   (I. i.)

Here indeed the prose is very similar in its rhythm and its figures to the prose of the "characters".

These are illustrations of a tendency towards the generalised utterance, which is indeed common in Jacobean drama as a whole but particularly so in Webster. We have only to turn over the pages of his plays to find many examples of the sententious line or passage preceded by inverted commas. Within

less than twenty-five lines of the scene where Vittoria
and Flamineo die, we have:

> *"Prosperity doth bewitch men seeming cleere,*
> *"But seas doe laugh, shew white, when Rocks are neere.*
> *"Wee cease to greive, cease to be fortunes slaves,*
> *"Nay cease to dye by dying.*

> *"While we looke up to heaven wee confound*
> *"Knowledge with knowledge.*

> *O happy they that never saw the Court,*
> *"Nor ever knew great Man but by report.*

> *"This busie trade of life appeares most vaine,*
> *"Since rest breeds rest, where all seeke paine by paine.*
>
> (V. vi.)

Often, as in some of these, the rhymed couplet is
used, which emphasises the semi-choric nature of the
utterance. When similar gnomic passages occur in
Shakespeare, they are either in soliloquy, thus standing apart from the play and functioning almost as
chorus-passages pure and simple, or they are used as
a means of deliberately lowering the dramatic tension.
For example, at the end of Act III of *Measure for
Measure* the Duke has a soliloquy of twenty-two lines
in octosyllabic couplets which begins as follows:

> *He, who the sword of heaven will bear*
> *Should be as holy as severe;*
> *Pattern in himself to know,*
> *Grace to stand, and virtue go;*
> *More nor less to others paying*
> *Than by self offences weighing.*

Shame to him whose cruel striking
Kills for faults of his own liking!
Twice treble shame on Angelo,
To weed my vice and let his grow! (III. ii.)

The passage is appropriately inserted at this point,
for the Duke has a little come down from his pedestal
in arranging the Mariana-device, and Shakespeare
apparently wishes to raise him once more to a sove-
reign and divinely sanctioned eminence: the remoteness of his speech from the manner of common
utterance, and its generalising tone, remove the
speaker from the other characters in the play and
make explicit the playwright's governing idea in the
drama. In *Othello*, I. iii, we find the Duke and
Brabantio exchanging flat, sententious couplets at
the point where Brabantio has despairingly with-
drawn his opposition to the marriage of Othello and
Desdemona: the dramatic interest is to turn to affairs
of state and the preparation for the Cyprus voyage,
and it is well for the tension to be momentarily
lowered. But in Webster the sententious passages are
commonly not thus separated from the action or used
for purposes of relief: they come in death-scenes, in
the final utterances of major characters. The result is
an effect of distancing when immediacy would be
better. Any dramatist undertaking a serious play will
have more or less consciously in mind a general view
of human life to communicate, but it will be most
successfully conveyed to us if its presentation is
largely indirect—especially at key-moments of the
dramatic action. Each of the tragic figures in Shakespeare's major plays dies thinking of his own con-
cerns—Hamlet of the succession to the throne of

JOHN WEBSTER

Denmark, Othello of his long service to the state, Lear of his hope that Cordelia is alive, Macbeth of his death-struggle with Macduff—and this makes their deaths more convincing, more eloquent than if their last words had the preacher's touch. Indeed, one of the reasons why the death of the Duchess of Malfi constitutes the most moving passage in Webster is that her thoughts, though incorporating a general truth, are concentrated on her own fate:

> *Pull, and pull strongly, for your able strength,*
> *Must pull downe heaven upon me:*
> *Yet stay, heaven gates are not so highly arch'd*
> *As Princes pallaces—they that enter there*
> *Must go upon their knees: Come violent death,*
> *Serve for* Mandragora, *to make me sleepe;*
> *Go tell my brothers, when I am laid out,*
> *They then may feede in quiet.* (IV. ii.)

On the other hand, the deaths in Act V of that play are liberally besprinkled with quotation marks. In this respect Webster is nearer to Chapman than to Shakespeare, and he is of course the lesser dramatist for that. But he differs from Chapman in that his generalised utterances are more commonplace, more an expression of a conventional morality: sin must be avoided, greatness corrupts, blood will have blood, man lives in ignorance, ambition is vanity—these are the sentiments which Webster's spent tapers illuminate in their last flash.

As *A Monumental Column* is an elegy on the hopeful Prince Henry, it inevitably contains its quota of "sentences", duly marked by inverted commas and sometimes by italics as well. But in other respects too the elegy throws light on Webster's character as a

112

poet. One of a number of verse tributes hurriedly
produced, it has little or no distinction. Its rhetoric
and its conceits are strained, as when the warlike
prowess of the Black Prince is alluded to: he, we are
told,

> *jestingly, would say it was his trade*
> *To fashion death-beds, and hath often made*
> *Horror look lovely, when i'th' fields there lay*
> *Armes and legges, so distracted, one would say*
> *That the dead bodies had no bodies left.*

Mr. Lucas is moved to describe these as "surely the
most detestable lines in all Webster",[1] and there is
indeed a strange lack of sensitivity here. When, as
often happens, physical horrors are mentioned in
The White Devil or *The Duchess*, it is with a proper
sense of the horrible. But in the later plays we have
already seen a strain of crassness, a blunting of sen-
sibility, a lack of discrimination which makes it
possible for the dramatist to end *The Devil's Law
Case* with the marriage of Contarino to Leonora, of
Romelio to his seduced nun. We should note too that
A Monumental Column was written just after the
probable date of *The White Devil* and earlier than
The Duchess of Malfi: we are not dealing here with a
product of Webster's later years. If, however, we
look back to his collaborations with Dekker, we shall
see in *Westward Ho!* and *Northward Ho!* a crudeness
of temper that cannot be solely Dekker's. I have
already referred to the madhouse-jesting of *Northward Ho!*, and both plays are full of dull cuckoldry
and duller threats of cuckoldry among the citizens
of London, interspersed with the self-congratulations

[1] Lucas, iii. 287.

of wives who decide to preserve their virtue. In fact, except on those occasions when Webster's mind is deeply disturbed by the human condition, it is a mind remarkable neither for sensitivity nor for nimbleness of thought. It is likely enough that he was to some extent affected by the death of the young Prince, but the experience did not set his mind working at top-pressure: he strained to impress, and the result is not merely conventional but tasteless. If it be objected that this is to apply too rigorous standards to a mere occasional poem, we may recall that *The Phoenix and the Turtle* was perhaps also written for a ceremonial occasion.

A Monumental Column illustrates, besides, a stylistic device common in Webster. That is the use of the barely relevant fable. He breaks off his lamentations over Prince Henry to tell how Pleasure once came down into the world and, when she was recalled to heaven by Jupiter, she left her robe behind: it was found by Sorrow, so that since then men "have entertain'd the divill in *Pleasures* cloaths". The fable takes up forty of the poem's 328 lines, and it is difficult to see how it relates to the brevity of Prince Henry's life. In *The White Devil*, IV. ii, when Vittoria and Brachiano are reconciled in the house of convertites and are about to depart to Padua, Flamineo interrupts the proceedings with a prose account of the crocodile, the worm that breeds in its teeth, and the bird that flies into the crocodile's jaws and removes the worm, escaping from the crocodile's ingratitude by wounding it with a "quill or pricke" that its head is armed with. Brachiano interprets this as a reproach that he has not rewarded Flamineo for his services, deducing that Flamineo is the bird and he himself the crocodile; Flamineo replies that Vittoria is the suffering crocodile, Brachiano the bird that relieves her: she is to beware of ingratitude. Both explanations are forced, and the second singularly pointless. Similarly, in *The Duchess of Malfi*, III. ii, Ferdinand, in the moment of great stress when he has entered his sister's bed-chamber and threatened her with his dagger, breaks off to tell how Reputation, Love and Death came into the world and were about to separate until Reputation said that, once he parted from a man, he was never found again. This, like the sudden intrusion of a gnomic passage, lowers the tension, and that was by no means the effect required here. We feel a lack of self-criticism, of mastery of the playwright's craft.

Webster excels in the sudden flash, in the intuitive but often unsustained perception. At times he startles us by what may be called the "Shakespearian" use of the common word. In the dark night of *The Duchess of Malfi*, at the high point of tension when the Duchess is about to die, her last words are:

> *Go tell my brothers, when I am laid out,*
> *They then may feede in quiet.*

The bareness of "feede" increases the force of the lines, for it suggests an animal's engrossment. It has too that kind of authority peculiar to the common word unexpectedly introduced. Its impact is like that of "bread" in Hamlet's

> *He took my father grossly, full of bread,*
> *With all his crimes broad blown, as flush as May;*
> (III. iii.)

115

and like that of "eat" in the last stanza of Herbert's
"Love bade me welcome":

> *"Truth, Lord; but I have marr'd them; let my shame*
> *Go where it doth deserve."*
> *"And know you not," says Love, "Who bore the blame?"*
> *"My dear, then I will serve."*
> *"You must sit down," says Love, "and taste My meat."*
> *So I did sit and eat.*

Webster indeed shares with the best of his contemporaries this gift of bringing the common word
fully to life.

In general it is his short rather than his long
speeches that impress us: we do not find in him, as
in Chapman, the elaborate development of an image,
the impassioned analysis of an idea; he has nothing
that we could put beside the splendidly rhetorical
defence of the actor's craft that Massinger gives us
in *The Roman Actor*. When he was "thinking things
out", his mind was not so different from the common
run. Compared with Jonson's or Chapman's, his
thought-processes were clumsy and of the surface.
He was no philosophical poet, and in his relaxed
moments had not even much feeling for the appropriate manner. When he deliberately aimed at the im-
pressive, he achieved often only the ponderous. He
was perhaps too easily influenced by other dramatists.
The White Devil and *The Duchess of Malfi* show him
at Shakespeare's feet, both in their general themes
and in the handling of particular scenes and speeches:
The White Devil stems from *Macbeth*, the tragedy of
unlawful action, as *The Duchess of Malfi* from *Lear*,
the tragedy of suffering; the scene of Cornelia's mad-

ness echoes passages from *Hamlet, Macbeth* and *Lear*;
the Duchess's momentary return to life is a clear
echo of Desdemona's. Later it was Fletcher who
became the dominant influence, and we can, if we
wish, blame him for the haphazard theatricality of
Webster's minor plays. Webster's two great tragedies come at the end of the splendid years of Jacobean
drama: they are almost the last illustrations of its
superb temper, the depth and frankness of its vision.
The stories of Vittoria and the Duchess kindled his
mind, and when writing these plays he had the
major work of his contemporaries to give him firm
footing. But new fashions were in the theatrical
atmosphere, and it was those that largely determined
the character of his later work. He had not that
authority of mind which enabled Jonson to plough
his individual furrow into the reign of Charles I.

Nevertheless, *The White Devil* and *The Duchess of
Malfi* are two of our major English tragedies. Perhaps Webster did not fully understand what he had
achieved, but that may be no uncommon charac-
teristic. Dramatists are rarely the wisest men of
their generation. Almost the best of them may say
more than they realise or wish, and leave blemishes
on their work which puzzle and distract us. Even
Shakespeare's feelings sometimes appear to run
counter to the governing ideas of his plays, as I
think in *Measure for Measure* and *The Tempest*, and
he has often scenes and speeches which we cannot
regard as helpful to the play's effect. But Shakespeare and Webster and lesser men are writers for the
theatre, where we have neither time nor inclination
for the sifting processes of chill criticism. In a
theatrical production we should treat a dramatist's

text with a discriminating respect, a respect proportionate to his stature. Webster's text is no more sacred than Shaw's will become. A serious dramatist is the principal artist of the theatre, but his utterance will not always be wise or skilfully contrived. He is no prophet, no complete philosopher, no omnicompetent magician. It would be as heinous to abbreviate Act IV of *The Duchess of Malfi* as it is to cut the "degree" speech from *Troilus and Cressida*, for in these passages the dramatists' minds are working at full pressure, are giving us moments of vision. But we should not deny that there is lumber in Webster, even in *The Duchess* and *The White Devil*.

But theatrical production can do more than prune these unequal masterpieces. They excel the general run of plays because of their passionately apprehended major characters and their superb flashes of great verse. The characters will live more surely if enacted by living players, the verse when spoken with the accent of authority will bite deeper into our minds. In mental stature Webster may stand lower than Marlowe, Jonson, Chapman, and of course Shakespeare; in craftsmanship Middleton may excel him, in emotional complexity Ford; but, Shakespeare alone excepted, Webster dominates the stage. He gives good parts to actors capable of them. His lines at their best are both majestic and intimate. He has a poet's fancy, and at times a poet's austerity. "Fate's a Spaniell, Wee cannot beat it from us." "I have caught an everlasting cold." "Looke you, the Starres shine still." These words demand the stage, as the Duchess demands a body of living flesh. In the theatre we have a sharper impression of the words and of those who utter them, we come closer to that vision of suffering humanity which Webster experienced in fits and starts. And when the fit was on him, his intuitions were sure and deep.

INDEX

INDEX

INDEX

DATE DUE